ST Training Solutions
Success Skills Serie

DAVID GOLDWICH

WIN-WIN
NEGOTIATIONS

DEVELOPING THE MINDSET, SKILLS AND
BEHAVIOURS OF WIN-WIN NEGOTIATORS

Marshall Cavendish
Business

Published by Marshall Cavendish Business
An imprint of Marshall Cavendish International
1 New Industrial Road, Singapore 536196

Other Marshall Cavendish Offices
Marshall Cavendish Ltd. 5th Floor 32–38 Saffron Hill, London EC1N 8FH • Marshall Cavendish Corporation. 99 White Plains Road, Tarrytown NY 10591-9001, USA • Marshall Cavendish International (Thailand) Co Ltd. 253 Asoke, 12th Flr, Sukhumvit 21 Road, Klongtoey Nua, Wattana, Bangkok 10110, Thailand • Marshall Cavendish (Malaysia) Sdn Bhd, Times Subang, Lot 46, Subang Hi-Tech Industrial Park, Batu Tiga, 40000 Shah Alam, Selangor Darul Ehsan, Malaysia

Marshall Cavendish is a trademark of Times Publishing Limited

National Library Board Singapore Cataloguing in Publication Data
Goldwich, David, 1959-
    Win-Win Negotiations / David Goldwich. — Singapore : Marshall Cavendish Business,
    c2010.
    p. cm. — (Success skills series)
    Includes index.
    ISBN-13 : 978-981-4276-61-0

    1. Negotiation in business. 2. Negotiation. I. Title. II. Series: Success skills series
    (ST Training Solutions)

HD58.6
658.4052 — dc22   OCN646005847

Printed in Singapore by Times Printers Pte Ltd

PREFACE

Congratulations on picking up this copy of *Win-Win Negotiations*. I'm very proud to include this in the ST Training Solutions Success Skills series. This series includes several short, practical books on a range of topics that will help you develop your skills and enhance your success at work and in your personal life too.

The Success Skills series was originally created to meet the needs of participants of ST Training Solutions public workshops. After attending our workshops, many participants expressed a real desire to continue learning, to find out more about the topic, to take it to another level. They were hungry for knowledge. Just the effect I hoped for when I set up ST Training Solutions in 2007. With the Success Skills series of books, the experience and expertise of our trainers can be enjoyed by many more people.

As Series Editor, I've enjoyed working with the authors to make sure the books are easy-to-read, highly practical, and written in straightforward, simple language. Every book is packed with essential tools and strategies that will make you more effective and successful. We've included illustrations throughout that reinforce some key points, because I believe we learn more if we add some fun and humour. You'll also notice some key features that highlight important learning points:

Myth Buster

Here you will find a statement that is not true, with notes on the true facts of the matter.

Fast Fact

Useful snippets of information or special points to remember.

Aha! Moment

This is a 'light bulb' moment, when we note something you may be able to conclude from a discussion. Don't forget to note your own 'Aha! Moments' perhaps when you receive some extra insight that clarifies an important point.

Try This

Here you'll find a suggestion for how you can put a special point into practice, either at home or at work.

Danger Zone

You'll find some words of warning here, such as things to avoid or precautions to take.

Star Tips

At the end of each chapter you'll find a list of Star Tips — important notes to remind you about the key points.

By picking up this book you have already shown a desire to learn more. The solid advice and practical guidelines provided in this book will show you how you can really go from good to great!

Good luck!

Shirley Taylor.

Shirley Taylor
Series Editor
CEO, ST Training Solutions Pte Ltd

www.shirleytaylortraining.com
www.shirleytaylor.com

Shape the Star in You!

Visit www.STSuccessSkills.com now to download your free e-book **'Your 7 Steps to Success'** containing motivating advice from our Success Skills authors. You can also read lots of author articles and order the latest titles in the Success Skills series.

CONTENTS

INTRODUCTION

We all negotiate every day, whether we realise it or not. Yet few people ever learn *how* to negotiate. Those who do usually learn the traditional, win-lose negotiating style rather than an approach that is likely to result in a win-win agreement. This old-school, adversarial approach may be useful in a one-off negotiation where you will probably not deal with that person again. However, such transactions are becoming increasingly rare, because most of us deal with the same people repeatedly — our spouses and children, our friends and colleagues, our customers and clients. In view of this, it's essential to achieve successful results for ourselves and maintain a healthy relationship with our negotiating partners at the same time. In today's interdependent world of business partnerships and long-term relationships, a win-win outcome is fast becoming the *only* acceptable result.

While we hear much talk about the coveted win-win outcome, this result is actually not common. Most negotiations will never result in a win-win outcome because of certain common negotiation mistakes and misconceptions. The win-lose mindset is so pervasive that it seems natural for many people. In this book, I hope to change this perception.

Win-win negotiators value their business and social relationships. They know that winning in a given negotiation is not as important as maintaining their winning relationships. Yet this does not mean that they must sacrifice their interests. Win-win negotiators believe they can win both the negotiation and the relationship. Most importantly, they understand that they can consistently achieve win-win results by developing and using a set of win-win negotiating skills and techniques.

You too can develop the win-win negotiator's mindset and learn the skills and techniques to successfully negotiate win-win agreements. The fact that you are reading these lines shows that you are interested in becoming a better negotiator — a win-win negotiator. As you continue reading, you will come to appreciate the benefits of the win-win mindset. You will find that the tools you need are not difficult to master. And you will realise that negotiating can be both fun and rewarding.

I hope you'll practise the skills and techniques shared in this book, and enjoy your journey towards becoming a win-win negotiator.

David Goldwich
www.reachforthestars.us
www.davidgoldwich.com

ASSESS YOURSELF

How much do you know about win-win negotiating?

1. Most negotiations will result in a _____ outcome:

a) Win-lose.

b) Partial-win, partial-lose.

c) Lose-lose.

d) Win-win.

2. The best way to negotiate a good outcome is to:

a) Play hardball.

b) Master tactics.

c) Prepare thoroughly.

d) Help your counterpart get what he wants.

3. A good way to achieve a win-win agreement is to:

a) Compromise.

b) Create value.

c) Trust your counterpart.

d) Focus on a single issue.

4. Compromise is:

a) The key to a win-win result.

b) The best way to break a deadlock.

c) Inadvisable, as it makes you appear weak.

d) Inadequate, as neither party gets what it needs.

5. It is important to support your position with:

a) Logic.

b) Passion.

c) Credibility.

d) All of the above.

e) Logic and credibility only.

6. You cannot get a win-win if the parties' positions are incompatible.

a) True

b) False

7. Tactics are:

a) Dirty tricks and have no place in a win-win negotiation.

b) The best way to negotiate a win-win agreement.

c) Necessary and expected in almost any negotiation.

d) All of the above.

8. In a difficult negotiation it is:

a) Better to negotiate the more difficult issues first. If you can't reach agreement on them there's no point in continuing.

b) Better to consider the easier issues first and save the more difficult issues for later.

c) Not important when you handle the difficult issues, so long as you deal with them.

d) Not likely to achieve a win-win outcome.

9. A deadlocked negotiation:

a) Is unlikely to end in an agreement.

b) Is not unusual, as most progress in a negotiation occurs towards the end.

c) Can be jumpstarted in many ways.

d) Answers b) and c).

10. No matter how many skills and tactics I learn, a hardball negotiator backed by greater resources and experience will win every time.

a) True

b) False

How did you do?

1. (b) is the correct answer. The most common negotiating outcome is a partial-win, partial-lose. This is because negotiated agreements are voluntary, and we wouldn't agree unless we derived some benefit (see Chapter 1). Thus, we would not usually agree to a win-lose or a lose-lose outcome. However, a win-win is rare, unless you know how to make it happen.

2. This one is a bit tricky, but the best answer is (c). Tactics are important, but preparation is paramount, as you will see in Chapter 1. Playing hardball makes reaching an agreement difficult. Focusing too much on helping the other party get what he wants is a sign that you may have an accommodating style of negotiating (see Chapter 2).

3. The correct answer is (b). Creating value is one of the keys to achieving a win-win result. Negotiating multiple issues also makes a win-win more likely — the more issues on the table, the more likely you are to reach a win-win outcome. While trust is important, it should not be given blindly. See the discussions on the win-win mindset in Chapter 2 and on currencies in Chapter 4. Skills, strategies, and a win-win mindset can also make a win-win agreement not only possible but likely. These major themes are discussed throughout this book.

4. I hope you chose answer (d). A compromise usually means neither party gets what they need. It is better to explore more options to create a win-win. Compromise only as a last resort. We consider the problem with compromise in Chapter 2.

5. Did you choose (d)? Obviously logic is important, but it is not enough. Credibility and passion are also important factors in a negotiation (Chapter 6). You should also be aware that emotions, biases, and a deep-seated need for procedural fairness can thwart even the most rational negotiator. Learn more about emotions and biases in Chapter 8.

6. The answer is (b) False — It is possible to satisfy the interests of both parties even if their stated positions are incompatible. We distinguish positions and interests in Chapter 4.

7. The correct answer is (c). All negotiators use tactics. While some can be quite harsh, others are expected. Negotiating tactics and counter-tactics are covered in Chapter 3.

8. While there is not universal agreement on this point, most negotiation experts would choose (b). It is usually preferable to begin with the easier issues. This allows you to get to know your counterpart and build trust and momentum, which will make the tougher issues easier to agree on. We look at building trust in Chapter 7 and dealing with an impasse in Chapter 10.

9. The best answer is (d). Don't give up hope when a negotiation stalls. There are many ways to overcome an impasse, as you will see in Chapter 10. And in most negotiations, the majority of gains are made towards the end.

10. This is (b) False — Anyone can learn to be a successful negotiator. This book will show you how!

SETTING THE STAGE

1

*"The man who is prepared
has his battle half fought."*

Cervantes

What is negotiation?

We all negotiate every day. We negotiate with our bosses and colleagues, our spouses and children, our customers and clients, people we sell to and people we buy from. We negotiate prices, goods, services, activities, schedules, and relationships. Negotiation isn't just for lawyers and wheeler-dealers. It's for everybody, including you.

There is no doubt that you realise this, otherwise you probably wouldn't be reading this book. You may also have some idea about what negotiation is. Rather than put forth a formal definition, let's take a look at some concepts embodied in the notion of negotiation.

1. Negotiation is a way of satisfying your interests, of getting what you need or want. We live in a web of relationships and interdependencies, and rely on others to help us. Similarly, others approach us to help satisfy their own interests. Negotiation is the barter system that streamlines these exchanges.

2. Negotiation is a form of persuasive communication. It is a way of getting others to do what we want them to do. As such, it requires us to use all of our communication skills: listening, asking questions, sharing information, interpreting information, framing proposals, reading body language, influencing and persuading. It requires empathy and understanding, knowledge and insight, diplomacy and tact.

3. Negotiation is an opportunity to solve a problem in collaboration with a partner. Unfortunately, most people think of negotiation as an opportunity to beat an opponent, to squeeze as much out of him as possible. However, when two or more people are squeezing at the same time, they are not likely to get what they want. This adversarial approach also does not bode well for any future relationship. If both parties can look at negotiation as a shared problem and strive to solve it together, they are both more likely to satisfy their interests.

Unfortunately, this is not the way most people approach negotiation, but my goal in writing this book is to help you change that mindset and become a win-win negotiator.

4. Negotiation is a process. Many people tend to think of negotiation as an event, where we sit at a table with someone, playing the negotiation game, trying to satisfy our own interests by squeezing or perhaps by engaging in collaborative problem solving. The truth is that negotiation begins sooner than we think. It begins as soon as we set out to satisfy an interest, and culminates in an agreement that ideally satisfies our interests fully. Do not confuse the grand finale — the handshake, the signing of the contract — with the work, research, and preparation that gets us there.

5. Negotiation is a game. It may not feel like a game, because we take it seriously. But it is a game, complete with rules — a game of skill and chance. If you learn to play the game more skilfully, you can reduce the effects of chance.

6. Like most games, negotiation is meant to be fun. A good negotiation well played can leave us feeling fulfilled and rewarded. But fun is in the mind of the player. With the right mindset, negotiation can be fun and rewarding indeed.

 Fast Fact

We live in a web of relationships and interdependencies, and we negotiate with others to help us get what we need or want.

Myth Buster

Negotiation is simply the art of bargaining or haggling.

Not so. It is much more than that. Negotiation is a process of persuasive communication that begins as soon as you recognise an interest that you cannot satisfy on your own.

Why negotiate?

We negotiate because we want something that we cannot get on our own. Someone else is in a position to give it to us or can help us get it. Alternatively, someone may be in a position to harm our interests, and we seek to dissuade them from doing so.

From this perspective, we are dependent on someone else. We feel weak, needy and at their mercy. We see our counterpart as having power over us.

What we may not see is that our counterpart also wants something from us, or he wouldn't be negotiating with us. We do not see how weak and powerless he feels as he deals with us, because he dares not show it. It's important to remember that we are also in a position to affect his interests in a positive or negative way. He needs us as much as we need him.

Consequently, we find ourselves in a web of relationships and interdependencies. We all need things from others, and we turn to one another for help. Negotiation is the process by which we help each other get what we need.

Possible outcomes

In any negotiation there are several possible outcomes.

- **Win-lose.** One party wins, and the other loses. This can happen when the parties are mismatched, or when one party is not prepared. It can also result from cheating. In any case, the loser will resent the winner, and any relationship between the parties will suffer. Still, we would all rather win than lose, and it is easy to see how this result could come about.

- **Lose-lose.** Both parties lose. You may be thinking, "How can that be? It's easy to see how one party might lose, but how can both parties voluntarily agree to lose? It just isn't rational!" You're right, it isn't rational. It is, however, surprisingly easy to become emotional in a negotiation, and one may agree to lose so long as he takes the other person down with him.

- **Partial win-partial lose.** Both parties get part of what they want, but neither has his interests fully satisfied. This seems fair since both come out better off than they were, and we all understand that we can't realistically expect to get everything we want. Or can we?

Fast Fact

A partial win-partial lose result is the most common negotiating outcome.

- **Win-win.** Both parties get everything they want! This is the best of all possible worlds! It's the ideal outcome. But while the win-win is much talked about, much sought after, and much prized, it is rarely achieved.

Why you need to be a win-win negotiator

Most seasoned businessmen learnt how to negotiate on the job. More often than not, they learnt an adversarial, old-school, win-lose style of negotiating. Their teachers were bosses and mentors who learnt adversarial negotiating from their own old-school bosses and mentors.

These win-lose negotiators see negotiation as a pie to be cut, and each of them wants the bigger slice. In other words, one person will win and the other will lose, so they do their best to win. As winning and losing is somewhat subjective, it becomes more apparent to them that they won when it is clear that the other lost. A loss for the other party is interpreted as a win for them.

This win-lose approach is only suitable for one-time transactions, where in all likelihood you will never see the other party again. In this situation, you probably don't really care if the other guy loses. You might care, though, if you believe in fairness, or karma, or if you want to maintain a good reputation in a world that is getting smaller and more interconnected by the day. In an isolated instance, however, most people just want to win.

But isolated, one-off negotiations are now the exception. Most of us must negotiate with the same people repeatedly over a long period of time, like colleagues, customers, vendors and partners. We need to achieve good results for our side while maintaining a healthy, long-term relationship with our negotiating partners. In today's world, a win-win outcome is fast becoming the only acceptable result.

Take a look at your computer. Aside from the manufacturer's brand, there are probably two or three other logos affixed to it, such as Intel or Microsoft. When Intel and the computer manufacturer negotiate the price of computer chips, do you think either company will accept a win-lose result? Of course not! They must have a win-win agreement.

I suspect that you too would like to have a win-win agreement in most, if not all, of your negotiations. With the tips found in this book, your chances of negotiating win-win outcomes will increase exponentially.

Aha! Moment

I need to be a win-win negotiator because I value my business and social relationships.

The negotiation process

I mentioned earlier that while negotiation is usually thought of as an event, it is in fact a process. This process begins the moment you perceive a want or need and set out to satisfy it. At that point you may not even be thinking about negotiating. You may not realise you are negotiating until you are actually bargaining with someone over how much it will cost you to meet that need. By then it is too late — your counterpart knows you need him and he knows you are unprepared. You've lost.

Preparation

In *The Art of War*, the Chinese military strategist Sun Tzu wrote, "If you know the enemy and know yourself, you need not fear the result of a hundred battles." In other words, preparation is the key to victory in battle. The same can be said of negotiation.

So how do you prepare for a negotiation? Most people who are preparing to negotiate to buy something will have in mind a very low price that they would love to pay, the highest price they are willing to pay, and a figure in the middle of that range, representing an estimate of what they expect to end up paying. Sellers go through a similar exercise. It's good to think about these expectations, but it is not enough.

You may imagine yourself a big shot negotiator and think you can just wing it. But understand this: real big shot negotiators do not wing it, they prepare. Here are some considerations to bear in mind in your preparation:

- Know thyself. What do you want? Not what you *think* you want, but what you *really* want. Surprisingly, many people are unsure of this. For example, you may think you want a raise in salary, and perhaps you do. But you might really want something else, such as recognition, to be treated fairly, to maintain or improve your standard of living, or to provide security for your future. A pay raise might do it, but there might be other ways of meeting your needs.

- Once you've determined what you want — or what you think you want — ask yourself why you want it. After asking yourself why a few times, you may realise you need something else after all. You cannot achieve a satisfactory outcome in a negotiation until you are clear about your real interests and goals, that is, what you want or need, and why you want or need it.

 Danger Zone

Do not assume that what you think you want will satisfy your interests. Ask yourself *why* you want it. You may discover another way to meet your needs.

- You will often find that you have multiple interests. You need to prioritise these. For example, in negotiating a position with a new employer, you might be interested in many things other than salary, such as insurance plans and other benefits, a flexible schedule, work environment, work assignments, team assignments, and so on. Some of these will be more important to you than others. It is unlikely that you will get everything you want. Prioritise your wish list into those items you must have, those you are willing to bargain for, and those that would be nice but not necessary. Then focus on your priorities and avoid being distracted by minor issues.

- Assess what resources you have, what you bring to the table. What do you have that your counterpart might want? These assets or 'bargaining chips' — anything of value that you might offer to exchange — are called currencies of exchange, or simply currencies. How can you value these currencies to justify your demands?

- What strategies and tactics might you employ in the negotiation? Will you make the first offer, or wait for the other party to do so? What concessions are you willing to make, and when? What is your time frame? What is your walk-away point? What is your Plan B?

All of this is a lot to think about, but we're not done yet! There are many other things you must consider:

- Know the other party. What does he want from you? Is he clear about his interests? What are his priorities? Does he really want what he says he wants, or does he have a hidden agenda?

- Anticipate your counterpart's negotiating style. Will he be a tough adversary or a collaborating partner? What is his negotiating strategy, and what tactics might he employ?

- Formulate some options. Based on your knowledge of what you want, the currencies you have, and your understanding of your counterpart's interests, begin putting together some options. An option is a possible solution to a negotiating problem. Create some options that will satisfy your interests as well as your counterpart's. Be prepared to present these options and discuss them.

- Know the environment. You and your counterpart will not negotiate in a vacuum. You will both be influenced by various factors. Some of these you can control, others you can only anticipate or respond to. The more you know about them, the better your prospects.

- Are there any relevant changes or trends in your respective industries? Consider how changes in interest rates or financial markets might affect your interests. What government policies or regulations might affect you or your counterpart? Does your counterpart have a business cycle you should know about? For example, car sales at the end of the month or toy sales before Christmas might provide an opportunity for you.

You can see that there is a lot to take into account before you negotiate. Gathering information is crucial in preparing for a negotiation.

Bargaining

After gathering information and preparing to negotiate, you will move to the main event: bargaining. This is what most people think of as negotiating. It may involve face-to-face discussions, phone calls, or e-mail exchanges. You and your counterpart will make offers and counter offers, explore options, test assumptions, clarify understandings, and hopefully reach an agreement that satisfies your respective interests. Just remember that the formal bargaining event is only part of the negotiating process. The outcome here depends largely on how well you have prepared.

Fast Fact

Negotiation is a process, it is more than just bargaining. The process of negotiation begins the moment you perceive a want or need and set out to satisfy it.

Timing issues

Timing issues are an important part of negotiating. You may feel that the clock is against you. This is because you are painfully aware of your own deadlines, sales targets, and other pressure points. You may not know what pressures your counterpart is under. Understanding a few principles about timing will give you confidence as a negotiator.

Most people tend to overestimate their own pressures and weaknesses, while assuming their counterpart has a stronger position than she really does. Do not assume you have it worse than the other party. They may just be playing it cool — wouldn't you?

Most progress in a negotiation occurs as the deadline approaches. This has two implications:

- If you don't seem to be making much progress early in the bargaining process, try not to fret. Continue bargaining and exploring options. Remind yourself that huge divides can be closed in a short time as the clock runs down.

- You can use deadlines to bring about progress. If you are in a rut, consider imposing a deadline to add a healthy dose of pressure.

There are two other points to consider about deadlines:

- Everyone has a deadline, even if you don't know it.

- The party with the least time constraint has an advantage over the one with a tight deadline. If you have a tight deadline, I suggest you keep it to yourself. However, do let the other party know you have a tight deadline if it may pressure them into reaching an agreement.

Aside from time deadlines, there are time scheduling issues to consider. You might be more focused in the morning than in the afternoon. You might not feel in the right mood for negotiating on a Monday morning, or you may be distracted by your weekend prospects on Friday afternoon. Your business — or your counterpart's — might be subject to weekly, monthly, seasonal or annual cycles that could affect the negotiation. Holidays could also be a factor. Be aware of the impact these time factors could have on your negotiation.

Venue and seating

When it comes to venue there are few rules, only guidelines. A good negotiator will consider all of these variables before deciding on an appropriate venue that will set the stage for the formal bargaining phase of the negotiation:

- Where should the negotiation take place? In your office or theirs? You may like the feeling of confidence and control that comes with the home field advantage, where you can choose the room and the seating arrangements and can manipulate the environment to project the image you desire. You also have your colleagues to back you up, as well as the administrative support of your staff.

- You may prefer to meet your counterpart in their own surroundings, where they feel more comfortable. This gives you the opportunity to observe them on their own turf and draw inferences about them. For example, does their organisation run smoothly or do they seem to be in disarray? What does the environment say about their financial condition and their ability to spend?

- You may choose to meet on neutral territory such as a restaurant or a hotel conference room. Meeting on neutral ground would help mitigate the effects of a home field advantage, and can also take you away from the distractions of your office. Would a formal or casual setting work better for you?

Seating

There is a reason why round tables are used whenever heads of state meet at an international summit — there is no head of a round table, so everyone appears equal. However, most corporate conference rooms have long tables, with a head and a foot. The head, obviously, is the power seat. It is reserved for the captain of the home team, and adds to his authority.

Perhaps you are sitting at a smaller table. Sitting opposite your counterpart at a table suggests an adversarial dynamic. After all, we play chess, table tennis, and other competitive games from opposite sides of a table. Sitting side by side, or kitty-corner, suggests both parties are attacking a problem together, from a common perspective. This sends a more favourable message. It is even better if the table is round. Better still is to consider sitting informally on a sofa or chairs around a coffee table, as this less intimidating informal setting will facilitate sharing, which might be more congenial to a frank discussion.

Setting the agenda

Develop an agenda before you sit down with your counterpart. The agenda should reflect the items to be discussed and their relative importance. Start with smaller or easier items to establish a pattern of success. Use this momentum to help carry you through the more difficult points.

Ideally, you should create the agenda yourself. Your counterpart may appreciate your taking on this extra work. It also gives you some control over the negotiation.

If your counterpart prepares an agenda, review it carefully to make sure it works for you. Keep in mind that it may have been crafted to afford him certain advantages. If you see anything you would like to modify, suggest a change and offer a reason for it. Even the agenda is negotiable!

Watch out if the other party tries to amend or deviate from the agenda during the negotiation. It is easy to lose track of items that are taken out of order.

Make notes on your copy of the agenda to aid your memory later. Even with the best of intentions, it is easy to forget a detail or the context of a discussion. Use your annotated agenda as the basis for a memorandum that you will draft shortly after the session.

Should you bring a team?

It's a good idea to bring a team, or at least one other person, to a negotiation whenever possible. Solo negotiators generally achieve substantially less favourable outcomes than those who negotiate as part of a team. Most people tend to perform better when others are backing them up, giving them confidence, and depending on them. Also, when you have others around, you have the benefit of multiple sources of experience, talent, and perspective. Two (or more) heads are always better than one.

Having a partner with you also allows you to use the good guy/bad guy tactic, which we will consider in Chapter 3. It also gives you a psychological edge.

However, do not bring your whole team. You will not be able to limit your authority if all the decision makers are present. Leave yourself an 'out' by making sure there is a higher authority not involved in the negotiation who you will need to consult for final approval.

What if your counterpart has a team and you don't? That could be intimidating. Remind yourself that negotiation is a voluntary process, and you need not agree to anything that is not in your interests. Be confident in knowing that you are prepared, and remember that they need you as much as you need them. And take heart in the knowledge that solo negotiators can often get even better results when they are outnumbered than when they negotiate one-on-one.

We have touched on some of the more important concepts of setting the stage for a win-win negotiation. In the next chapter we will build on this foundation and explore the mindset of the win-win negotiator.

Star Tips for setting the stage for negotiating

1. Remember that we live in a web of relationships and interdependencies, and we negotiate with others to help us get what we need or want.

2. Treat negotiation as a process rather than as mere bargaining.

3. Consider the negotiation to begin the moment you perceive a want or need and set out to satisfy it.

4. Achieve more win-win outcomes in your negotiations by preparing thoroughly.

5. Begin gathering information as early as possible. This is the most important part of preparing to negotiate.

6. Use timing to your advantage. Understand that most progress in a negotiation occurs as the deadline approaches.

7. Ensure the right negotiating environment. Venue and seating arrangements may seem incidental, but they can be important in negotiating a win-win agreement.

8. Achieve greater success in your negotiations with a team approach. You will be more successful in a team than on your own.

9. Learn to achieve win-win results consistently. These outcomes are not common, but they are becoming increasingly necessary in today's interconnected world.

10. Learn to play the game of negotiation more skilfully. Negotiation is a game of skill and chance. With more skill, you can reduce the effects of chance.

THE WIN-WIN MINDSET

"You don't get what you deserve, you get what you negotiate."

Chester Karrass

2

Win-win negotiators are found in the same places as win-lose and lose-lose negotiators. They are not any more experienced, and they look about the same as well. The big difference between win-win negotiators and all the others is their mindset.

Win-win negotiators understand the five styles of negotiating and are able to adapt to their counterpart's style and to the situation. They choose to exhibit certain positive behaviours and avoid negative ones. They are optimistic, open minded, and collaborate with their negotiating partner to solve their problem together. In this chapter we'll take a look at the qualities of a win-win mindset in detail.

Five styles of negotiating

There are two dimensions that determine negotiating style: assertiveness and people orientation.

Assertiveness is the ability to communicate your interests clearly and directly. It is the ability to stand up for yourself without stepping on anyone else's toes. Assertive people are able to ask for what they want, say no when they need to, and state how they feel in any situation. They also accept standards of fairness and recognise the rights and interests of others.

People orientation denotes a sensitivity to the needs and feelings of others. It encompasses empathy, emotional awareness, and ease in social situations. Those with a high people orientation are generally sociable and likeable. They are people driven rather than task driven.

Your negotiating style is a function of how assertive you are and how people oriented you are, as illustrated in this diagram:

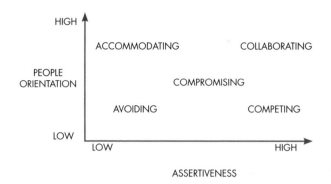

Avoiding

A person with an avoiding style of negotiating avoids the issues, the other party, and negotiation situations as much as possible. An avoiding negotiator

- avoids confrontation, controversy, tense situations

- avoids discussing issues, concerns

- puts off negotiating whenever possible

Accommodating

The accommodating negotiator is primarily concerned with preserving his relationship with the other party, even at the expense of his own substantive interests. An accommodating negotiator

- focuses on the other party's concerns more than his own

- helps the other party at his own expense

- tries to win approval by pleasing the other party

- follows the other party's lead

- emphasises areas of agreement

Competing

The competing style of negotiating is characterised by an emphasis on self interest and winning at the other party's expense. A competitive negotiator

- uses power to effect a more favourable outcome

- exploits the other party's weaknesses

- wears the other party down until he gives in

- may use threats, manipulation, dishonesty, and hardball tactics

Compromising

The compromising style places a premium on fairness and balance, with each party making some sacrifice to get part of what it wants. A compromising negotiator

- splits the difference

- believes in quid pro quo, give and take

- seeks a solution in the middle of the range

Collaborating

Negotiators with a collaborating style seek an optimal outcome by focusing on mutual interests and trying to satisfy each other's needs. A collaborating negotiator

- deals openly and communicates effectively

- builds trust

- listens to the other party

- exchanges ideas and information

- seeks creative solutions

- strives to create value

- sees negotiating as an exercise in joint problem solving

Avoiding and accommodating negotiators generally do not fare well in negotiations. They tend to be soft and are not comfortable being firm. They need to be more assertive. Preparing thoroughly may inspire confidence. Having an assertive colleague present during negotiating sessions would be a good idea. But a course on assertiveness training and practice developing assertiveness skills would be recommended.

Competitive negotiators look for a win-lose result. It would be wise for them to help their counterpart win as well. After all, they still win, and they also gain goodwill by allowing their counterpart to enjoy a victory. However, competitive people often prefer to see their counterpart lose; for them, it reinforces the idea that they have won. It is not pleasant dealing with a competitive negotiator, even if you are assertive. However, you will need to negotiate with such a person on occasion. The best you can do is to understand him, brace yourself, and try to find a win-win. He may not begrudge you a win if he wins as well, but he is only concerned with his own interests.

Compromising negotiators, at first glance, appear reasonable. They are willing to give up something in exchange for something else, provided their counterparts do the same. Some people even define negotiation as the art of compromise. However, I feel this approach does the art of negotiating a disservice. As we will see shortly, it is the easy way out. It is far better to use the ways of the win-win negotiator than to settle for half a loaf.

Collaborating negotiators,   as you have probably concluded, are win-win negotiators. They work with their counterparts to solve their problem together by building trust, communicating openly, identifying interests, and designing options that allow them to create value for all involved.

When to use each style

The collaborating style of negotiating is clearly the win-win approach. If we are advocating the win-win approach and learning win-win techniques, why bother with the other four styles? There are a few reasons.

- While you may be sold on the merits of win-win negotiating, your counterpart may not see it that way. You will find yourself dealing with competitive types. You need to recognise that style and know how to protect yourself.

- Even committed win-win negotiators can use other styles. Sometimes you will be expected to be competitive, or to compromise. Remember, negotiation is a game. You need to understand and play by the rules.

- No single style is good enough for all occasions. You will need to be flexible enough to adopt other styles.

Most people have a dominant or preferred style, but it may vary with the situation and the people involved. While collaboration is generally the best outcome, and avoidance and accommodation are not usually effective, there are times when each style has its advantages.

Consider choosing an approach based on these factors:

Avoiding

When the issue is trivial, it may not be worth your time. When emotions are running high, it is wise to avoid negotiating for the time being. However, this is a temporary measure. Avoidance is a poor long-term strategy.

Accommodating

When the issue in question is not important to you but is important to the other party, you may choose to let them have the point. This is an easy concession to make in exchange for something else later. Ideally, you should ask for something on the spot in exchange for your concession.

Competing

In a one-off negotiation where you have no ongoing relationship with your counterpart, you may not care whether he wins or loses, you just want a win. Or in a negotiation where the only issue is price, a gain for one party means a loss for the other. The most likely result when negotiating solely on price is a partial win for both parties. However, few negotiations are only about price. Finally, you may find yourself negotiating in a crisis situation that requires quick, decisive action on your part.

Compromising

You may find yourself in a situation where time pressures require a prompt settlement, and you don't have the time to explore win-win solutions. Or where both parties are equal in power and neither will concede much. Or where the parties accept a compromise as a temporary measure to a complex problem, and intend to pursue a more lasting settlement later. You might also compromise when neither party can propose a win-win solution and both prefer a partial win to no deal, although in such cases it would be best to put in more effort and try to come up with more imaginative options.

Collaborating

When both parties want a win-win and have the time and mindset to pursue it, the chance of a win-win is good. Or the issue may be too important to compromise, and failure is not an option. When a win-win is imperative, there is usually a way to get it.

Myth Buster

A collaborating style is the only one needed in win-win negotiations.

This is not true. While collaboration is the ideal, even win-win negotiators need to use other approaches on occasion.

The problem with compromise

When two people can't quite close the gap and reach an agreement, it is common to compromise. One person might say "Let's just split the difference," or "Let's meet in the middle." He believes this is the fair thing to do, as each party is making a sacrifice and each is getting part of what he wants. No matter how fair it may seem, however, it is not good negotiating.

The Old Testament tells a story about two women, each claiming to be the mother of an infant. Both women approached King Solomon to resolve their dispute. He suggested that they cut the baby in half, knowing that the real mother would prefer to see her child alive with someone else than dead in her own arms. Sure enough, he was right — King Solomon was known for his wisdom, after all! Imagine if the two women did agree to split the baby. That would definitely have been a lose-lose outcome. But a compromise often is.

When we compromise, both parties make a sacrifice. While each gets something, neither gets what he wants. Compromising usually leads to a partial win at best, never a win-win.

A better way is to consider more options and try to find a win-win. Sure, it takes more effort. But we often compromise far too quickly, without really trying to find a win-win solution.

It's best to accept a compromise only as a last resort. There may be times when a compromise really is the best you can do. But more often than not, you can find a way to achieve a win-win outcome. It may take time, perseverance, creativity, and a good flow of communication, but the results will be worth it.

 Danger Zone

While compromise is often used to resolve difficult negotiations, it is a cop-out. Exhaust all efforts to collaborate on a win-win before taking the easy way out.

Attitude is the key

The most important tool a win-win negotiator has is his attitude. A win-win negotiator is positive, optimistic, collaborative, and objective. He understands that a win-win outcome is rarely an accident, but the result of systematic application of certain principles. These principles are:

• Approach the negotiation as an opportunity to engage in joint problem solving with your counterpart. Think win-win instead of win-lose. Look for ways to enlarge the pie so everyone gets a bigger piece.

• Treat the negotiation as a game. Learn the rules and practice the skills. Have fun and try to improve over time. Play the game.

• Be objective. Don't fall in love with the subject of the negotiation. Be aware of the roles of emotion and biases. Take calculated risks.

• Be positive and optimistic. Aim high. Set an aggressive anchor and justify it.

• Be persistent. Continue generating options and looking for ways to create value. Compromise only as a last resort.

• Keep your Plan B in mind and be prepared to exercise it.

 Myth Buster

A good attitude is just a bunch of New Age hype.

Wrong! While skill is important, your attitude has a strong impact on your negotiating results.

Five characteristics of win-win negotiators

This diagram shows the five characteristics that all win-win negotiators share:

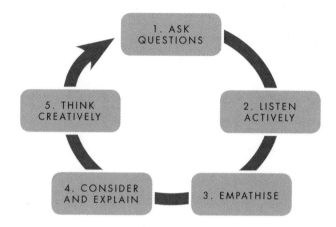

Let's take a look at each of these characteristics in detail now:

Ask questions

Win-win negotiators ask a lot of questions. While asking questions is a good way to get the information that is critical for a win-win, this is not the only purpose served by asking questions. Asking questions helps you build rapport, gain thinking time, control the discussion, clarify understanding, and persuade the other party. Of course, it is also a good way to gather information. Asking questions will help you to:

- **Build rapport.** People generally engage in small talk when meeting someone new, or when encountering someone they haven't seen in a while. They usually ask mundane questions or make simple statements that invite response. "How are you?" "Nice weather we've been having." "Think it'll rain?" "Did you see the game last night?"

These questions are not designed to elicit useful information. No one cares about the weather except farmers, and I can poke my head out the window and see if it looks like rain myself. We ask these trite questions just to acknowledge that another human being is present, to interact with him at a basic level, to put him (and ourselves) at ease.

A win-win negotiator will ask questions and make small talk to be friendly and to get his counterpart to warm up to him. He wants to be likeable. He knows that other people are more likely to agree with him if they like him. Cold and aloof negotiators do not fare as well as warm and friendly ones.

- **Gain thinking time.** Asking questions is a good way to buy time. While the other party is responding, you can ponder a difficult point. Try to do this during pauses in the conversation, as you don't want to miss anything important while you are thinking. Use questions to slow down the pace of the negotiation and gather your wits.

- **Control the discussion.** If you have ever observed a trial lawyer conducting a cross examination, or an interrogator grilling a suspect, you know how questions can be used to control a conversation. You can ask the questions you want to steer the conversation in the direction you want, to follow your agenda. It's better to be the one asking the questions than the one in the hot seat.

- **Clarify understanding.** Win-win negotiators ask questions to test their assumptions and confirm their understanding. Ask a direct question if you are not sure about something, even if you *think* you are pretty sure about it. Better safe than sorry.

- **Persuade the other party.** We negotiate to persuade another person to do what we want him to do. People often react defensively when confronted with a direct statement. For example:

    "I think I'll have the last donut." [Direct statement]

    "Hey, I was going to have it!"

Instead, use leading and rhetorical questions gently to suggest the answer you want.

"You weren't going to eat the last donut, were you?"
[Leading question]

"Um, no, you can have it."

"Do you really need all those empty calories?"
[Rhetorical question]

"You're right, I don't."

Of course, there are no guarantees that you will get the answer you want, but using questions skilfully is more persuasive than telling people what you want them to do.

- **Gather information.** Open questions encourage free-flowing conversation. There are many possible and unpredictable answers. While open questions may elicit the information you were seeking, they often yield additional, unanticipated, and potentially valuable information as well. They open up the field of inquiry, providing a wide variety of information for you to explore. For this reason, open questions are especially useful in the early stages of a negotiation.

Closed questions usually yield a simple "Yes" or "No." Closed questions are good for establishing facts, confirming understanding, gaining commitment, and summarising. Thus, they are most useful at the later stages of a negotiation.

 Aha! Moment

Open up the negotiation with open questions, and close with closed questions.

Follow-up questions may be either open or closed. They allow you to gather additional information and detail.

When asking questions, be careful with the tone of your voice, the way you phrase your questions, and your body language. A sigh, or the sound of impatience or exasperation in your voice, can put the other person on the defensive and cause them to yield less information. Use a warm, friendly tone when probing, for that will help you to get the answers you want.

Be especially careful with a naked "Why" question. A "Why" question can sound like an accusation, and puts the other party on the defensive. Find a way to turn it into a "What" or "How" question. For example:

> "Why did you do that?" [sounds harsh, accusing]

> "What made you decide to do that?" [sounds softer, more sincere]

Listen actively

Effective listening is perhaps the area of communication that is most taken for granted. Most of us believe that because we have a good sense of hearing we are therefore good listeners. Nothing could be further from the truth.

Hearing is a passive, physiological process that occurs when your brain registers the impact of sound waves on your eardrum. Listening, on the other hand, is the more active process of interpreting the sounds we perceive and giving them meaning. Listening requires *thought*.

Western cultures value speaking over listening. We think more highly of men of words and action than those who sit quietly. Our companies reward those who express their opinions, not those who weigh the opinions of others. No wonder most of us prefer to speak than listen. This is not necessarily a good thing in a negotiation.

You already know what *you* want from a negotiation (or at least you should). Wouldn't it be great to know what your counterpart wants? Wouldn't that help you in formulating possible solutions to your negotiation? If so, you need to listen and learn. And in particular you need to listen actively.

Effective listening is often interpreted to mean active listening. And while empathetic listening is an even higher level of listening, active listening is a great start. Here's how to listen actively:

- **Paraphrase.** Restate or paraphrase what the speaker has just said to test assumptions, clarify confusion, and confirm understanding. Seek to completely understand the substance of the message. Use phrases such as

   "If I understand you correctly ...."

   "What you really want is ...."

   "Am I correct in saying that you ...."

- **Encourage the speaker.** Use statements, words, or sounds to encourage the speaker to continue or elaborate:

   "I'd like to hear more about that."

   "Why is that?"

   "Really?" "No kidding!" "Unbelievable!"

   "Hmmm." "Uh huh!" "I see."

You can also use non-verbal signals to encourage the speaker, such as nodding your head in agreement, exhibiting appropriate facial expressions, leaning forward, maintaining an open and attentive posture, and mirroring the speaker's body language. Your objective is to get as much information as possible, and to understand your counterpart clearly.

- **Focus on red flag words.** Red flag words are ambiguous words or phrases that cry out for elaboration. For example, the word "interesting" can mean "intriguing", or it can be a diplomatic way of saying "I don't like that idea much." When someone uses the word, seek clarification.

People choose their words for a reason. If you are not sure what they mean, ask them. Your counterpart may use certain words to avoid giving information. Learn to recognise these red flags and dig for the information your counterpart is reluctant to share. If you ask specifically, he will often tell you. For example:

> *"That's a very interesting proposal, Mr. Jones. However, I feel we could manage with our current configuration for the time being."*

You should be thinking, and asking: "What do you mean by 'manage'? Is it not doing everything you expect? What is working well, and what would you like to see improve?" You could also seize on the phrase "for the time being" by asking, "How long are we talking about? What is your time frame? What other factors are affecting your time frame?"

 Aha! Moment

I need to learn to spot red flag words and uncover the valuable information lurking behind them.

Empathise

The only problem with active listening is that it can be mechanical. Animated figures at Disneyland also nod their heads in agreement and say, "I see." An active listener may be sincere, or she may not be. Sometimes it's hard to tell.

Empathetic listening includes all of the elements of active listening discussed above, plus another element: reflecting the speaker's emotional state. Knowing what others are feeling and showing them that you care is the essence of empathy. You must truly understand a person's feelings to reflect them — you can't fake it! Take your active listening to an even higher level. Strive to become an empathetic listener. Here are some keys:

- Show empathy by identifying your counterpart's feelings and reflecting them. It isn't enough to care about the person — you must *show* her that you care.

- Make statements and ask questions that reflect your counterpart's emotional state. For example:

  "That must have been a big disappointment."

  "I can see that you're frustrated."

  "You must be worried about that. What are you going to do?"

This does wonders towards building rapport and trust, strengthening your relationship, and encouraging the flow of information. It also makes you more likeable.

- Note that empathising does not mean agreeing. You can understand how your counterpart feels without agreeing with her position. She will appreciate your concern whether you agree with her or not.

 Aha! Moment

People don't care how much I know until they know how much I care.

Consider and explain

Most negotiators reject an offer or proposal without giving it much thought. Perhaps they respond immediately with their own counter offer. They feel they are projecting confidence and strength by exhibiting such a clear grasp of what they want and don't want. They fear that any hesitation on their part will be considered a sign of weakness by the other party.

Win-win negotiators know better. An immediate rejection is insulting. It shows a lack of respect. That offer is a product of — and an extension of — the other party. You do yourself no service by behaving rudely towards your counterpart. By pausing to consider an offer, you show you are taking both the offer, and the other person, seriously.

Also, by thinking about your counterpart's offer, you just might find some merit in it. You may find some common ground that you would otherwise miss with an out of hand rejection. After considering the offer, explain what you like about it and what you don't like. Finding even a shred of value in his offer and working with it will place you in higher regard with your counterpart than if you had rejected his offer completely. Remember, win-win solutions depend on collaboration and joint problem solving, not on prevailing in a contest of ideas.

Finally, give a reason why you don't like the offer. People like to know why. It makes your rejection easier to accept. It also helps your counterpart understand your needs and interests, improving the likelihood of a win-win solution.

Think creatively

Average negotiators come up with obvious solutions. Win-win negotiators think creatively. The win-win is often hidden, lurking behind positions masquerading as interests, and is not easily spotted by average negotiators. It requires creativity to uncover a win-win solution. Creative thinking helps us to:

- **Identify interests.** It is not always easy to identify our own true interests, let alone our counterpart's. What we think we want may not be what we really need. Sometimes we have to think out of the box to see the difference.

- **Identify currencies.** Currencies are sometimes hard to identify. Because we do not value a certain asset that we possess, we may not realise that our counterpart finds value in it. We may not even know that it exists. Creative thinking helps us remove our blinders.

- **Generate options.** There may be many countless potential solutions to a negotiation. We may only think of one. Or we may think of a few, decide one is the best, and not realise that there may be even better ones out there. The more options we can generate, the more likely we will find one that presents a win-win solution. Creative thinking helps us generate more options.

- **Recognise patterns.** Precedents, accepted practices, norms, and other patterns are easy to see. They provide us with shortcuts. We follow the pattern and it makes our life easier. At least it does most of the time. However, if you do the things other people do, you will get the results other people get. If you want something better — such as a win-win — you need to do things better. Creative thinking helps you decide when to follow patterns and when to break them.

 Try This

Practise solving brain teasers and other puzzles. This will help you to become a more creative thinker.

A win-win negotiator is distinguished by his mindset. He understands the five negotiating styles, he recognises his own strengths and weaknesses, and he takes steps to compensate for those weaknesses. He is flexible and knows when to adapt his style. He asks questions, listens actively and empathetically, and considers proposals carefully, explaining what he likes and dislikes about them. He is also creative in generating options.

As we will see in the next chapter, the win-win negotiator also understands a wide range of negotiating tactics and is able to respond with the appropriate counter-tactic.

Star Tips for developing a win-win negotiating mindset

1. Learn to recognise and adapt to the five styles of negotiating.

2. Remember that collaborating is the key to a win-win, but other styles have their time and place.

3. Resist the urge to compromise. Compromise is easy, but it isn't a win-win outcome.

4. Maintain a win-win attitude. Be positive, optimistic, collaborative, and objective.

5. Ask questions not only to gather information, but also to build rapport, gain thinking time, control the discussion, clarify understanding, and persuade the other party.

6. Listen actively to confirm understanding and encourage the speaker.

7. Listen for red flag words and uncover the valuable information lurking behind them.

8. Empathise with your counterpart, even if you don't agree.

9. Say what you like and don't like about an offer before making a counter offer.

10. Think creatively to identify interests, currencies and options.

NEGOTIATING TACTICS AND COUNTER-TACTICS

*"Force, no matter
how concealed,
begets resistance."*

American Indian proverb

3

Tactics are a part of nearly every negotiation. If negotiation is a game, tactics are the plays, the parries and thrusts. For every tactic (offensive manoeuver) there is a counter-tactic, or defence. If you want to be a great negotiator, you will need to be familiar with a wide range of tactics, and you must also know how to defend against them with an appropriate counter-tactic.

Negotiation is a game, and as in most games there are many different tactics and counter-tactics. You need to be able to juggle them around and choose the best ones for any given situation.

Why do we need tactics?

In Chapters 1 and 2 you have seen many reasons why I am advocating win-win negotiation, which is also called 'principled negotiation'. Some of the hallmarks of this style of negotiating are joint problem solving, effective communication, trust, fairness, and maintaining healthy and mutually rewarding long-term relationships. The relationships issue is key here because we are, in essence, negotiating with partners rather than adversaries.

With all of these high-minded ideals, you may be wondering, "Why bother with tactics? Aren't tactics just a bunch of dirty tricks?"

Have you ever noticed that, in a bargaining situation, sellers tend to ask for a higher price than they are willing to accept? And that a buyer's first offer is usually less than he is willing to pay? It's a classic example of the old dictum 'Buy low and sell high'. This highball and lowball opening gambit is one of the most frequently used negotiating tactics.

As this simple tactic is so common, we almost expect to encounter it whenever we bargain. In fact, we would find it hard to believe that an opening bid could be anyone's true bottom line. Consequently, when we hear the opening price stated, we naturally begin to bargain. No doubt our counterpart would respond in the same way.

Remember, negotiation is a game. Some tactics are expected, even between such intimate negotiating partners as husbands and wives. We are expected to use certain tactics as part of the game.

There is another reason why you need tactics and counter-tactics. You are learning how to become a win-win negotiator. However, your counterpart may be an old-school, adversarial negotiator. She may use tactics against you, so it's important that you are able to recognise and counter them.

Negotiation tactics are not always black and white, fair or unfair, ethical or unethical. There is a lot of grey. You need to be prepared for whatever may come your way.

Myth Buster

Win-win negotiators are above using tactics.

This sounds noble, but it's not true. Everyone uses tactics. Not all tactics are dirty tricks, and some tactics are expected — they are part of the game.

Initial offers and counter offers

As we've just seen, most negotiations involve a dance around high and low opening offers and counter offers. If you want to dance, you need to learn the steps.

No one expects a first offer to be a best offer. This is one reason why you should never accept an opening offer. You know your counterpart is highballing or lowballing. You know you can negotiate for a better offer, and it would be foolish not to.

But there is another reason you should not accept a first offer. It would make the other person feel he had been taken advantage of.

Imagine you are at a neighbour's yard sale and see a wonderful antique cabinet. You ask the owner how much, and he replies $200. Immediately, you say "I'll take it!" and whip out your wallet. The seller would have been willing to accept less after a little give and take. When you quickly agreed to his first highball offer, he was surprised. Now, he feels that you know something he doesn't and got a fantastic deal, and he is a sucker. Even though you accepted his price, he feels like he was on the losing end of a win-lose transaction. He expected to play the game, his expectations were not met, and he is dissatisfied. Your neighbour would probably resent you, and the bad feeling could impact any future relationship.

On the other hand, suppose you had counter-offered $150, and ultimately agreed on $175. You would have gotten a better deal, and the seller would feel that he got a fair price. His expectations of haggling and meeting in the middle would have been satisfied, and he would be happy. Never accept the first offer.

Try This

Even if you are delighted with their first offer, express some reluctance. Your counterpart will feel better.

Who goes first?

The opening offer and counter offer dynamic is simple to understand. More complicated is the question of *who* should make the opening offer.

Some people feel it is better to open the negotiation themselves. Others advocate never making the first move. Which is correct? There is evidence in support of both positions. Let's consider each approach.

Approach #1: Let the other party make the initial offer whenever possible

Your counterpart's initial offer might be more favourable than you expected. It might be better than anything you would have dared to ask for. If so, good for you. But remember, don't accept a first offer immediately. Haggle a bit so your counterpart feels like a winner. People are more satisfied when they work for it.

You learn something when your counterpart makes the first offer. Regardless of whether the first offer is high or low, it tells you something about your counterpart's mindset, aspirations, confidence, and perhaps his sense of reality. It gives you a bit more information about him before you begin bargaining.

If the initial offer is not favourable, you can start bargaining. Even if you do not like his first offer (and there is a good chance you won't), you can always make a counter offer and begin bargaining. You have nothing to lose by listening, as long as you heed the next paragraph.

If the initial offer is way out of line, dismiss it firmly but politely. Do not respond to an unrealistic offer. Flinch (see page 51) and explain that you really cannot respond to such an offer, then wait for something more reasonable. Once you make a counter offer, you have in effect legitimised his initial offer, which becomes an anchor point for the entire negotiation. That first offer, combined with your counter offer, establishes a negotiating range. Chances are that any agreement will be somewhere near the middle of that range, and how favourable that middle figure turns out to be will depend on the first figure from your counterpart that you respond to.

As you can see, there is ample support for letting the other party make the initial offer. Let's consider the alternative.

Approach #2: Make the initial offer yourself

The initial offer is a powerful anchor. It establishes one end of the negotiating range, and thus influences the settlement price. It is to your advantage to set the initial anchor point yourself, rather than allow your counterpart to do so.

Your initial offer should be at the high end of your aspiration range, and within or close to your counterpart's acceptable range. As you will probably have to make concessions anyway, it's best to start from a high figure and make your counterpart work for any concessions. Don't give anything away before you begin bargaining.

However, you don't want to start out too high. Try to set a high anchor, but a realistic one. If you set it too high you could lose credibility, and your counterpart will resent you. Make sure your initial offer is attractive to you and something your counterpart could conceivably accept.

It's usually good practice to use an odd number. Exact figures look as if they were calculated according to a precise mathematical formula and have an aura of permanence about them. It is harder to dispute an odd number than a nice round figure that looks as if it was made up without any thought.

Imagine a salesman saying "$10,000 is my absolute bottom line." Would you believe him? Probably not. You'd wonder why not $9,999.95 or $9,990? If he had said "I can't go a cent below $9,987.64" you might think he had sharpened his pencil as much as possible, and you would probably accept the figure without question.

Support your offer with reasons, but invite and be open to their counterproposal. Once you have presented your initial offer — an odd figure from the high end of your aspiration range — explain why that figure (which probably seems high to your counterpart) is fair. Ask him what he thinks, and listen attentively. Wait for his counter offer and carry on from there. Just remember that if his initial counter offer is unrealistic, do not allow it to take hold as an anchor point.

There are certain situations where it is especially advantageous for you to make the first offer. If it is a complicated negotiation with many elements other than price, your proposal becomes the benchmark. Your counterpart may use your proposal as the basis for future discussion, a reference for comparison with his own ideas. Your offer sets the tone for the negotiations that follow.

Other tips for making offers and counter offers

- Do not appear too eager for a deal. If the other party senses you want it badly, she will make you pay dearly for it.

- Do not get emotional about the subject of the negotiation, for example, a house or a car. Remember, there are plenty of fish in the sea. Focus on your objective of getting what you want at a fair price and on good terms.

- Do not make a counter offer too quickly. A counter offer is a rejection of the previous offer. People take rejection personally. When the rejection is immediate and without apparent thought, it can be taken as a sign of disrespect. Take some time to think about every offer, especially when it is a complicated proposal rather than a simple price. People like their ideas to be taken seriously.

- Give reasons when making a counter offer. Tell the other party what you like about their offer and what you would like to change, and why. People like to know why.

- Be prepared for any response, and control your reaction. You never know what the other party might say or do. Whatever the response, maintain your composure. Wear your poker face.

- Get offers and counter offers in writing. Putting it in writing makes your offer seem more official and persuasive. People take written words and figures more seriously than spoken ones. Writing also protects against memory lapses, genuine or otherwise.

Anchor points

The first offer in a negotiation and the ensuing counter offer serve as anchor points. These are reference points that we use because we like to make comparisons. We use them as starting points when considering whether to accept an offer or what counter offer to make.

Other references also serve as anchor points. The list price of an item at retail is perhaps the best known. Have you ever been impressed with an item's 'sale' price as compared with its regular price? Taken on its own, a sale price may not be attractive by any objective standard, but when compared with a higher figure it looks appealing.

A list price, a bid price, the price of a similar item, or a previous price for a similar or identical item can also be seen as anchors. An anchor draws us to an arbitrary figure and makes the eventual settlement price appear more attractive by comparison.

We use references and comparisons as short cuts. However, if you've ever walked down a dark alley late at night you know that short cuts can be dangerous. By relying on an anchor point, we suspend our objectivity. And we do rely on anchor points all the time, even if they have no basis in reality. A number thrown out at random, completely unrelated to the subject of the negotiation, can affect the settlement price in the negotiation. And while you may make some correction when evaluating anchor points, it is commonly not enough.

The important thing is to understand how anchor points work, and be vigilant against their effects. This example may help.

> *Imagine you are on holiday on some exotic tropical island. A local approaches you in the market with a string of beads made by the natives. "Good morning sir. Would you like to buy this beautiful necklace? The usual price is $30, but for you, only $15." You might think you're getting a huge discount and take it. Or you might remember that you should never accept a first offer, and make a counter offer of $10. In that case, you may end up buying the necklace for about $12 or $13. Or you might counter offer $5, in which case you would probably end up paying about $10 if you decide to buy it. If the initial pitch had been "Usual price is $30, but for you, only $20," you would have paid more, depending on your counter offer. The price you agree on is a function of the anchor points.*

	Scenario A	Scenario B	Scenario C	Scenario D
First offer	$15	$15	$20	$20
Counter offer	$5	$10	$10	$15
Probable settlement	$10	$12–13	$15	$17–18

Our discussion of initial offers, counter offers and anchor points yields a few rules:

- Always ask for more than you expect to get.

- Always offer less than you think the other party will accept.

- Never accept the first offer.

- Be aware of anchor points, and don't let your counterpart set an unrealistic anchor.

Fast Fact

Anchor points determine the negotiating range and influence the settlement price.

The flinch

The flinch is another classic manoeuvre that we all expect. When done well, it works — even when we know the tactic is being used!

The flinch, or wince, is when you express shock or surprise at an offer. The intent is to send a message that the offer is oppressive, in the hope that the offerer will retract his extreme offer and replace it with a more reasonable one. In this way you get an immediate concession without making one yourself.

A flinch

- creates doubt in the mind of the offerer.

- can help prevent an anchor from being set.

- may cause the offerer to improve his offer before you respond.

How do you counter a flinch? When your counterpart flinches, do not respond with a better offer right away. Instead, explain why you feel your offer is fair. Now you are discussing the offer, which legitimises it and helps it take hold as an anchor. If you choose to moderate your offer, your counterpart will have worked for it, and perhaps made a concession. You will not have reduced your offer unilaterally.

Reluctance

I suggested earlier that you should never appear too eager for a deal. It's always best to play it cool. When you express reluctance you are essentially 'playing hard to get'. As in love, feigned disinterest often makes the suitor work harder to win you over.

The squeeze

You can often squeeze further concessions out of your counterpart without making a concession yourself simply by responding with a comment such as, "You'll have to do better than that" or "You need to go back and sharpen your pencil."

If this tactic is successful, your counterpart may improve his offer beyond your expectations. If not, you can continue the negotiation from there.

The counter-tactic to the squeeze is to reply "How much better?" Now, the squeezer is on the spot and needs to commit to a figure. If you are the squeezer, anticipate the use of this counter-tactic and have a specific figure in mind. If it is not accepted, continue negotiating as before.

Good guy/bad guy

You've seen this in the movies: the bad cop intimidates the prisoner, then the nice cop comes in. The prisoner confesses to the nice cop, thinking he will be better off dealing with a 'friend'. He focuses on the stylistic differences between the good and bad guys, overlooking the fact that they are both on the same team and have the same objective.

This happens in business negotiations as well. The roles can be played by a team of negotiators, a businessman and his attorney, or even a husband and wife making a major purchase. It is an effective way of pressuring the other side into making bigger concessions.

The counter-tactic to this ploy is to expose the culprit. Let them know you are on to them and tell them you don't want to play games. Just say it in a good natured way.

 Danger Zone

Watch out for the good guy. He may seem nice, but he's still on the other side!

Timing as a tactic: deadlines and delays

Timing is an important element of any negotiation. Either party can manipulate the clock to his advantage.

One party might impose a deadline to rush the other party to action. "The 50 per cent off sale ends tonight. Tomorrow this bedroom set will go back to its usual price."

Or a party may drag his feet, hoping to prompt his counterpart into offering hasty concessions. "Well, I'm not sure, I'd like to think about it..."

Timing is a pretty intuitive matter to employ. You just know when it would serve you to speed things up or slow things down. On the other hand, it is not always easy to see when your counterpart is manipulating the clock, nor is it obvious how to handle it.

Here are two things you need to know about timing tactics so that you can deal with them effectively:

- Deadlines are usually arbitrary. They are set just to get you to act. You can always negotiate a change in a deadline. Even court and tax filing deadlines can be extended!

- The counter-tactic to a timing tactic is to do the opposite.

If you feel pressure from a looming deadline, ask for more time. If your counterpart cites policy, ask to speak with a higher-up. Explain that the negotiation is important, and both parties deserve adequate time to consider the merits. The bedroom set will still be there in the morning.

If you feel the negotiation is dragging on, impose a deadline yourself. Remind your counterpart that you have other alternatives, and need to decide by such and such a time.

NEGOTIATING TACTICS AND COUNTER-TACTICS 55

Competition

It's sometimes a good idea to casually let your counterpart know that you are talking with other parties and considering other alternatives. Let him know that he has competition and will have to win your business. Remember, never appear too eager for a deal.

Your counterpart also has alternatives, in the form of your competitors. Remind him of what makes you unique, whether it's your quality, reputation, experience, or some other differentiating factor. Remind yourself that he is negotiating with you for a reason.

Authority limits

Whenever you negotiate, it's always a good idea to limit your authority. Having someone to check with is convenient when the other side is pressuring you for a commitment you may not want to make. Perhaps you are not as well prepared as you thought, or would like more time to think it over.

Car salesmen use this tactic all the time. After hearing your offer they disappear to "check with their manager", then return to tell you their "hands are tied".

Many people let their egos get the better of them during a negotiation. They may say something like: "I'm the boss, I can do whatever I want, I don't need permission from anybody." Once you have said that, the other party may press you to agree to a proposal you may be unsure about.

But what if you really are the boss, and the other side knows it? There is no one higher you can defer to. So what can you do? You can defer to someone *lower* than you. For example, you can say, "I'll have to check with my accountant before I commit to that figure," or "I need to run that past my marketing team and get back to you." As the boss, you would do well to delegate certain responsibilities to others you trust, and it is only natural to value and rely on their input.

Some negotiators like to ascertain at the beginning of the negotiation that they are dealing with a person with decision-making authority. This is a good practice. However, if they try it with you, don't take the bait. Tell them you have authority to a point, and will need to check with others beyond that point. Do not name a specific person, or they may want to get his approval on the spot. Your higher authority should be a vague entity, such as a committee, management, or the Board of Directors.

Negotiations are unpredictable. Always leave yourself an out. Even if you don't use it, you will be more comfortable — and confident — just knowing it's there.

Silence

Most people are uncomfortable with silence. During an awkward pause, they say something — anything — to break the tension. This is usually a mistake.

Learn to be comfortable with silence. Let the other party do the talking. She just might say something that is music to your ears.

Suppose your counterpart makes a concession. You remain silent. She is wondering what you're thinking, and might assume you feel her concession is inadequate. As the silence becomes uncomfortable, she opens her mouth to speak — and offers you a bigger concession. She is now negotiating with herself.

If your counterpart clams up on you, don't give anything away. Repeat your last comment, ask her what she thinks about it, read through your papers, stare her in the eyes, or excuse yourself to make a phone call or use the restroom. Do anything to break the dynamic without conceding more. Just make sure you don't break into nervous giggles.

Bundling

You walk into a fast food restaurant for lunch. You order a burger and a medium drink. Then you notice that you can get the same burger and drink *with fries* for just a bit more. It seems like such a bargain. When you stop eating and stare at the remaining piece of burger and fries that you can't finish, you wonder why you ordered so much food. You've been bundled!

Sellers often bundle a set of related items at a special price to entice you to spend more. Sometimes it is a bargain, like when you really do want a burger, drink, and fries. Often it is just a tactic to separate you from your money.

To counter the bundling tactic, focus on your interests. Determine which items in the bundle you want and which you do not want. Negotiate for a package that includes only what you want. Do not be swayed by a package of unnecessary extras just because it looks like a good deal.

 Aha! Moment

> I can avoid paying for unnecessary extras by focusing on my interests.

Star Tips for using negotiating tactics and counter-tactics

1. Understand tactics not only so you can use them, but also so you can defend against them with the appropriate counter-tactic.

2. Weigh the pros and cons before deciding whether to make the first offer.

3. Never accept a first offer.

4. Aim high when making an opening offer, but don't insult the other party.

5. Understand that initial offers and counter offers can serve as anchor points. They establish the negotiating range and strongly influence the settlement price.

6. Play hard to get by using the flinch and reluctance tactics. This often results in a sweeter deal.

7. Use the clock to your advantage, but remember that most deadlines are arbitrary.

8. Limit your authority. Allow yourself an out by being able to defer to others on certain points.

9. Be comfortable with silence. Don't blurt out something you'll later regret simply because the silence feels awkward.

10. Watch out for bundles. Accept only the items you want.

POSITIONS, INTERESTS, CURRENCIES AND OPTIONS

"Sometimes one pays most for the things one gets for nothing."

Albert Einstein

4

Positions versus interests

One of the keys to reaching a win-win agreement is to understand the difference between positions and interests. Although the terms are often used interchangeably, they are not the same.

- **Positions** are the demands and offers made by the parties in a negotiation.

- **Interests** are what the parties consider most important to them — what they truly need, or *why* they want it.

Simply stated, a position is what you say you want, while an interest is what would actually satisfy your needs. Believe it or not, many people think they know what they want, yet they may not be aware of what their real interests are.

It may help you to think of interests and positions as parts of an iceberg. Positions are the tip of the iceberg that you can see, while most interests are hidden beneath the surface.

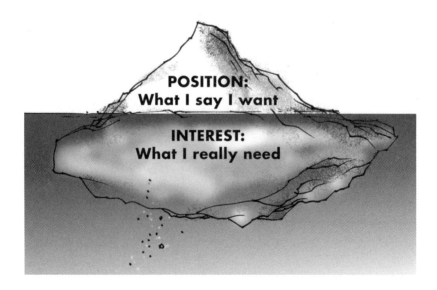

POSITION:
What I say I want

INTEREST:
What I really need

Danger Zone

Don't confuse positions with interests. People don't always know what they want. You need to look beneath the surface to discover what they really need.

For example, suppose you ask your boss for a raise. Your boss tells you that he would like to grant your request but there is no money in the budget for a raise. You then either quit your job for one that pays better and hope you like it as much as your previous job, or you continue to work unhappily while the resentment builds. Nobody wins.

Do you really need a raise? Or is that simply your position, that is, what you think you want? Why do you want a raise? What is your real interest? It's probably not the money itself, but some means of maintaining or improving your lifestyle. While a raise could help you satisfy this interest, there are also other ways to satisfy it. A company car, health benefits or a housing allowance might serve the purpose as well. Your boss might be able to satisfy your interests through one of these means, even if a raise is out of the question.

A position may be a means to satisfy an interest, but it is not necessarily the only — or the best — way to do so.

Focusing on positions is not productive. It often leads to interests being overlooked. If you advance your position of wanting a raise, your boss will defend his position of being unable to give you one, and neither of you consider other options that might address your interests.

People become attached to their positions. If they abandon or change a position, they appear wishy-washy and lose face. Defending your position can be against your interests, yet you may not notice it as you strive to project strength and consistency. This can get personal and damage the relationship between the parties.

Danger Zone

You must resist getting bogged down in positions. Instead, focus on your interests, that is, what is most important to you. It's also important that you can satisfy the interests of the other party, at least in part, or they may not continue to negotiate with you.

Identifying interests

For each position advanced by you or your counterpart, you need to ask: "Why? What purpose does it serve?" This enables you to uncover the underlying interest behind each position. A rule of thumb is to determine whether there is more than one way to satisfy a demand. If not, you are dealing with an interest.

For example, you may want a pay raise as a form of recognition by your company of your value and contribution over the years. There may be other ways of getting the recognition you crave: a new title, a promotion, more perks, or additional responsibilities. Thus your opening position might be "I want a raise," but your true interest might be "I deserve more recognition."

You may have heard an old story about two sisters squabbling over an orange. Each sister clings to her own position, which is that she is entitled to the orange. Obviously they cannot *both* have the orange. Eventually, after much argument, the sisters reveal their true interests. One wants orange juice, and the other wants to grate the rind to flavour a cake.

The sisters' original positions are incompatible and mutually exclusive. If one gets the orange, the other doesn't — a win-lose outcome. Or they can do what most fair-minded people will do: compromise! They could cut the orange in half, so each gets something but neither gets what she wants. Perhaps half an orange does not yield enough juice to satisfy one sister's thirst, and does not have enough rind to flavour a cake.

Only by identifying and sharing their interests do they find a way for each sister to get everything she wants.

Myth Buster

Incompatible positions can make agreement impossible.

Not necessarily. Even when positions are incompatible, both parties may be able to satisfy their interests 100 per cent.

You may think that the story of the squabbling sisters is quaint and contrived, and that nothing like it could ever happen in the real world. It can and it does, and for very high stakes.

In 1979, Egypt and Israel signed a peace treaty. A major stumbling block to the agreement had been the disposition of the Sinai Peninsula. Historically part of Egypt, it was captured by Israel during the Six Day War in 1967. Israel insisted on retaining all or part of it, while Egypt demanded the entire area. The positions were clearly incompatible.

Agreement was reached only after both parties' interests were addressed. Israel did not really want the land per se; it wanted the security buffer the land provided. Egypt did not require all of the attributes of sovereignty; it only wanted its traditional patrimony to be made whole. It was willing to demilitarise portions of it to achieve its main interest. Israel returned the land in exchange for security guarantees, and both parties' interests were satisfied in full — a win-win.

Prioritising interests

Make a wish list of all the things you could possibly get out of a negotiation. For each item, ask yourself "Why?" (perhaps more than once) to determine your true interests. Prioritise them so you are clear on which are most important to you. For a simple negotiation it might be enough to create three categories: high, medium and low priorities, or the three categories may be: what you must have, what you really want, and what would be nice to have.

It is tempting to say, "Everything is important to me! I want this and this and that!" But not everything is equally important. To be more realistic and disciplined about your priorities, list all of your interests. Then assign each interest a numerical weight such that the weighted value of all your interests totals 100 points. This will help you focus your attention on what matters to you most. It will protect you from exchanging good value for something trivial while forgetting all about your main objectives.

Try to anticipate the other party's interests and priorities as well. You may not be able to rank them with precision, but you could probably determine which ones he considers very important, somewhat important, or of low importance.

Sharing information about interests

It's amazing how secretive people can be during a negotiation. They seem to feel that anything they say can and will be used against them. As a result, they don't share information, which makes it difficult to uncover their true interests.

There is clearly some information you may not want to share. You might be tight lipped about your bottom line, your budget, your deadline, and so on. However, it is usually best to make your interests known.

What harm could have been done if one of our squabbling sisters had said "I need the orange because I want to grate the rind for my cake"? Chances are the other would have replied "Is that all? I only want a glass of orange juice." Problem solved.

Once you disclose your interests, the other party will often reciprocate. But what if they don't? Will that put you at a disadvantage? The answer is no. Sharing information about interests is a key to a win-win, even if the other party does not reciprocate. By making your interests known, they are more likely to be satisfied. You need not agree to anything that does not satisfy your interests, and knowledge of your interests by the other party can help her find a way to satisfy them.

Currencies

Make a list of everything you have that your counterpart might want. These items are called currencies. Of course, the best known currency is money. There is also the product or service the money is being exchanged for. But there are many other currencies, including method of payment, delivery schedule, other terms and conditions, brand and reputation, allocation of risk, timing, emotional needs, perceptions, and anything else of value. Note that it isn't just about price.

Then think of everything your counterpart has that you want, and prioritise this list as discussed above.

Then, and most importantly, think of everything you have that your counterpart might want. I mean everything. Your counterpart may have many needs that are not readily apparent, including emotional and intangible ones. The more of these needs you can identify and offer to meet, the more value you have.

 Fast Fact

A currency is *anything* of value. Currencies may be tangible or intangible. Money is only one of many currencies. A win-win negotiator *always* looks beyond price.

I often ask the participants in my negotiation workshops whether they would like to negotiate with Donald Trump. Most smile nervously as they say no. "Why not?" I ask, although I already know the answer. They do not believe they would fare well in a negotiation with the tough, intimidating and business-savvy Trump.

A few, however, raise their hand to indicate that they would like to do a deal with Donald. Their reasoning is usually that they may not make the best deal, but they would learn from the experience.

I suggest there is another reason: it would be a great story to tell future negotiating partners. Imagine... You're in the middle of a negotiation, and you say, "This reminds me of a deal we made with Donald Trump a few months ago. We agreed to..." Your negotiating partner is now thinking, "Wow! This guy did a deal with Donald Trump? I'm impressed — he must *really* be a bigger big-wig than I thought! I've *got* to close this deal." It would be great for your reputation — and your ego — to be able to drop Trump's name in this manner. And you can be sure Trump knows this, and factors it into his negotiating demands!

You may not be a celebrity like Donald Trump. But you might be able to identify other hard-to-recognise currencies and extract added value from them.

We don't always want the same things

It is easy to assume that others see things as we do. After all, we are rational, successful, and must have done something right to end up where we are today. Surely we know what is right, good and important. If we want something, everyone else must want it too. If we value something, others must as well.

Of course we all see things differently. One sister sees an orange and wants juice, another sees it and wants to bake a cake. One values the juice and has no use for the rind, but the other needs the rind and doesn't care about the juice.

One country wants land, and another only wants security.

One employee wants recognition, and another only wants more money.

We all have our own idea about what we want, and that's a good thing. It gives us a better chance of finding a win-win solution.

The problem is our mistaken assumption that others are like us. We need to learn that others are different and recognise these differences.

Aha! Moment

Not everyone thinks like me. The fact that others may value things differently creates an opportunity for a win-win.

Creating value from differences

Somewhere in the wilderness, a cow defecates. This waste product, as the term implies, has no value to the cow. A farmer stumbles upon the dung. He thinks to himself, "I can use this dung to make bricks and build a house. I can use this as fuel to cook my dinner and warm my family. I can use this to fertilise my crops and improve my livelihood." To the farmer, this waste product is like gold.

Closer to home, a restaurant manager ponders what to do with her used cooking oil. She could dump it in the alley, creating a stench and risking a citation from the health inspector. She could pay a waste removal company to dispose of it. Or, she could sell it to a company that converts used oil into fuel.

One man's trash is another man's treasure. At times you will find that you value something far more than the other party, and vice versa. This is an ideal opportunity to create value. If you can give the other side something it values highly at little or no cost to yourself, you can get a lot of mileage out of it. Perhaps they can do the same for you. Now you each give up a little to gain a lot. This is a key to reaching win-win agreements.

Property tycoon Donald Trump tells of a particular piece of property he wished to purchase, but the owner A was asking far too much. In negotiating another deal, Trump learned that his counterpart B had an option to purchase the coveted parcel from A at a much lower price. As B no longer wished to exercise the option, it was worth little to him — but it was very valuable to Trump! Trump paid a higher price to B than he would have otherwise paid because B included the option, which Trump then exercised to get a much better deal with A. Trump and B had a win-win based on a differently valued asset.

To identify items that may be valued differently by the parties, here are some things to consider:

- **Perceptions:** Some people will pay more to save face, look good, or have their ego stroked. They will pay a large sum for a shirt with a designer's logo stitched onto it, even though the same shirt may be available without any logo for much less. The perception of value is important, though it varies among individuals.

- **Risk:** People have different risk profiles. Some people are risk averse, while others boldly accept risk. A more risk averse party may be willing to concede more if her negotiating counterpart is willing to assume certain risks involved in the transaction. People buy insurance from companies that absorb risk, and insurance companies themselves routinely buy and sell allotments of one another's portfolios to share risk.

- **Combining similar resources and skills to achieve economies of scale:** There is power in size, and there is power in numbers. Two or more parties can pool their demand to negotiate more favourable rates from suppliers. For example, a number of small independent grocers can band together to obtain lower prices from a food producer.

- **Combining different resources and skills to accomplish together what neither could do alone:** Entities with complementary attributes can create synergy. For example, a landowner and a building contractor can form a joint venture to develop the property and get a better return than either might have otherwise enjoyed.

By exchanging currencies that are valued differently, each side can get more by giving up less! What painless concessions can you make that might be valued by the other party? What might they easily do for you that would be of great value to you? By focusing on interests and exploiting differently valued resources, you are more likely to attain a win-win outcome.

Options

The purpose of negotiation is not to convince the other side to let us have what we want. It is to help make each of us better off than we would have been otherwise. It is to solve a problem jointly for mutual benefit, rather than to compete for gain at the other's expense.

An option is a possible solution to a negotiation. It is one of a range of possible sets of currencies.

The solution to the negotiation puzzle — whether we are better off than we would have been without negotiating — is a function of the choices available to us, that is, our options. The more options we have, and the better they are, the greater the likelihood that one will be a win-win.

Returning to the case of the two sisters and the orange, what were their options? How could they have solved their problem? Sister A could have let Sister B have the orange, or Sister B could have let Sister A have it. They could have cut the orange in half in a misguided attempt at compromise. They could have tossed a coin or drawn lots to decide ownership. They could have fought over it. They could have bid for it. They could have brought in other currencies (a banana, strawberries, choice of which programme to watch on TV) and agreed on some distribution of all the fruit (and control of the remote). Ultimately, they found the win-win: one squeezed out the juice and the other grated the rind.

The sisters had quite a few options, and there are no doubt others we haven't considered. Most of them were win-lose or partial win solutions. Only one was a win-win. Most of the options, although unsatisfactory, were easy to conceive. The win-win was more challenging.

Our three favourite options

Most negotiators begin with three options in mind:

- The best deal I can get

- The worst deal I will accept

- The most likely agreement I believe we can reach

There are several problems with this range of options. First of all, you don't really know what the best deal you can get is. You may have certain expectations based on your assumptions about what your counterpart has and wants, and within the context of your necessarily limited world view. There might be something better for you and you might not even see it because you are locked into your original position.

Similarly, you can't be sure of the worst deal you will accept. You may have a bottom line price in mind, but the introduction of other currencies could influence you to change that. For example, you may decide that the lowest price you will accept for your widgets is $0.93 per unit, but you may be willing to accept less if the buyer pays cash, or takes delivery at your factory, or orders an unusually large volume, or if he also buys some monogrammed widget covers, among other possibilities.

Furthermore, having this limited range of options in mind may give you false confidence that you are prepared, and it is essential to prepare for a negotiation in the face of uncertainty. However, this is not the way to prepare. It would set a range based on arbitrary positions rather than interests.

Start generating options by listing and prioritising your interests, then listing all of your currencies. List your counterpart's interests and currencies as best you can. Remember, options are possible solutions to your negotiation. Currencies determine your options.

Creating options from currencies

To prepare well for a negotiation, you must first understand what you really want. You'd be surprised to find how many people are not even sure of what they want.

Next, try to anticipate what your counterpart wants. You may never be sure of what he wants, but with a little foresight and research you can get a pretty good idea. Remember to test your assumptions later during your discussions.

Finally, combine these currencies into a range of packages, or options. The more interests and options you have on the table, the greater the chance of a win-win agreement.

By focusing on options that promote interests rather than positions, we can create more value for each side. Each party may offer certain currencies to induce the other party. Recall that *an option is one of a range of possible sets of currencies.*

Option 1: Party A offers currencies A, B, C. Party B offers currencies X, Y, Z

Option 2: Party A offers currencies A, D, F. Party B offers currencies V, Y, Z

Option 3: Party A offers currencies A, D, E. Party B offers currencies W, X, Y, Z

And so on.

Any option (set of currencies) is a potential solution. Obviously, you would prefer to offer the smallest, cheapest and easiest currencies that would be acceptable to the other party.

Some negotiators believe you should never offer a currency or make a concession without getting something in return. Others believe that offering a unilateral concession can help advance a stalled negotiation. The first approach is sounder. If you feel tempted to make a concession to overcome an impasse, offer the concession in exchange for something else, for example, "I would be willing to offer X in exchange for Y."

If you do make a unilateral concession, do not make another concession without getting one in return. Two in a row will signal your counterpart to ask for more.

 Aha! Moment

Concessions are currencies. Even small concessions have value and should not be given away freely.

Star Tips for understanding positions, interests, currencies and options

1. Understand the difference between a position and an interest. A position is what you say you want, while an interest is what you really need.

2. Look beneath positions to uncover interests.

3. Be clear about what your interests are, and prioritise them.

4. Anticipate your counterpart's interests; do not accept his positions at face value.

5. Do not look only at price. A currency can be almost anything of value.

6. Try to identify all of your currencies. Do not overlook anything of value.

7. Look for ways to exchange differently valued currencies. This makes a win-win easier.

8. Options are possible solutions to your negotiation. Currencies determine your options.

9. Identify multiple interests, currencies, and options to maximise the chance of a win-win.

10. Always ask for something in return when making a concession. Concessions are currencies. They have value.

DEVELOPING AND USING YOUR PLAN B

"You got to know when to hold 'em, know when to fold 'em, know when to walk away and know when to run."

Kenny Rogers, "The Gambler"

One of the main themes of this book is that you must prepare well for a negotiation. So far we've discussed how you need to gather information, study the negotiating environment, consider your interests and currencies, anticipate your counterpart's interests and currencies, formulate a strategy, understand and anticipate tactics and counter-tactics, and develop a range of options. While this is excellent advice, it is no guarantee that you and your negotiating partner will reach a satisfactory agreement.

You have limited control over the process and eventual outcome. There are just too many variables that you cannot control. Information is limited and imperfect. Situations change. Strategies and tactics fail. Emotions, ego, and irrationality affect human behaviour. All you can do is your best.

And have a backup plan.

Always have a Plan B

Whenever you prepare to negotiate, ask yourself how you could best satisfy your interests if you and your negotiating partner are unable to reach an agreement. Could you satisfy your interests somewhere else? If so, with whom? Under what terms and conditions? Before you begin to negotiate, always have a viable backup plan, or Plan B.

Suppose you are engaged in a difficult negotiation. Your counterpart is driving a hard bargain, and you are beginning to feel that you may have to settle for less than you would like. What can you do? The answer depends on your Plan B.

Negotiation is a consensual process, based on mutual agreement. You do not have to accept any offer unless you choose to. You can always say "no". But we negotiate to satisfy some interest, and if we do say "no" we must find another way to satisfy our interest.

In everyday jargon we use the terms 'option' and 'alternative' interchangeably. In the negotiation context, however, it is useful to distinguish between options and alternatives. An option is a possible solution to a negotiation. During a negotiation there is often a range of options or possible agreements available to satisfy your interests. But if you and your negotiating counterpart cannot agree on one, you may have to look elsewhere for an alternative means of getting what you need. These alternatives exist outside of the negotiation.

For example, suppose you are negotiating for a salary increase with your current boss at Myco. You and your boss have a number of options available: she can offer you a big increase, no increase, or an increase of any number of figures in between. She can base the increase on your performance, the cost of living, or tie it to company practices or industry trends. She can offer you various combinations of benefits in lieu of a higher salary. These are all options that can result in a negotiated agreement.

If you and your boss cannot reach an agreement, you still have a choice: you can accept what your boss offers, or you can resign. What, then, are your alternatives? How can you satisfy your interests (recognition of your worth, maintaining your standard of living, being treated with fairness and respect, among other things) outside of Myco? You can find a position with another company, change careers, resume your studies, retire early, start your own business, or run away and join the circus. You may not like any of these alternatives, but you do have choices.

Some of your alternatives are better than others. When evaluating the options available with your negotiating counterpart, you just need to know which of the various alternatives available to you is the most attractive. This is your Plan B. You then choose between what your counterpart is offering you and your Plan B. In the example given, if your best alternative is to find a similar position with another company, you can forget about joining the circus for the moment. Your decision then becomes: should I accept my boss's offer and stay with Myco, or do I take a job with Other Company?

If Other Company has not offered you a job, then you do not have that alternative. Your best alternative then might be to start your own business. If that is not particularly attractive to you, you would do well to find a better alternative. If you have no good alternatives when you ask your boss for that raise, you will have little power in the negotiation. You will have to accept what she offers, or resign.

The power of a strong Plan B

Without a backup plan you have very little negotiating power. With an attractive alternative you have great power, even if your counterpart is a large, wealthy corporation. What traditionally passes for power — money, resources, an impressive title with a large organisation, and other trappings of power — are no guarantee of success in negotiation. Other sources of power, such as information, preparation and expertise, can tilt the balance of power in favour of the little guy. An attractive alternative is perhaps the greatest source of power of all. This source of power is largely a function of information and preparation.

Your Plan B is critical for a number of reasons:

- **Your Plan B gives you confidence.**   Your Plan B is like a safety net. If you can get a better outcome in the negotiation, take it; if not, walk away from the table and go with your Plan B. It *guarantees* that you will not be worse off by negotiating.

- **Your Plan B is a benchmark.**   Most of the time, your Plan B is not very different from an option on the negotiating table. For example, your Plan B may be an offer for a position with Other Company at $3,500 a month and you are negotiating with Myco for a similar position at a comparable salary. Knowing your Plan B gives you an idea of what a realistic option should be.

- **Your Plan B must be realistic.**   It should be something you could and would really do if the negotiation fails. Bluffing, that is, claiming to have a Plan B that does not exist, can be risky. If you are negotiating a salary increase with your boss at Myco and you tell her that Other Company has offered you $1,000 more, she just might say "A thousand dollars more? That's great! You *should* take it!"

Don't deceive yourself by fantasising about an alternative that you wouldn't actually exercise. For example, suppose you have no competing offer and you decide your best alternative is to start your own business. That would require capital, a business plan, a considerable amount of effort, a healthy bank balance to tide you over for several months, some quantum of risk, and so on. If you are not prepared to accept these challenges, this is not your Plan B. Stop dreaming, and develop a realistic Plan B.

- **Your Plan B can be improved.** Your Plan B is not fixed. For example, suppose your Plan B is an offer for a position with Other Company at $3,500 a month. All things being equal, you would not accept an offer from your boss for less than that figure. If Myco offers you $3,600 you take it; if they offer you less you go with Other Company. But what if, during your negotiations with Myco, you contact Other Company and they agree to increase their offer to $3,800 plus insurance coverage and a transportation allowance? Or you get an offer from ThirdCo at $3,900? Now you can confidently ask Myco for more, knowing you can beat their previous offer of $3,600. Once you determine your Plan B, see if you can improve on it.

Aha! Moment

Having a Plan B will give me confidence and guarantee that I will not lose.

The danger of your bottom line

In Chapter 4 we saw that many negotiators decide upon the 'worst' deal they are willing to accept before they begin negotiating. The rationale is that it is better to think about this coolly and objectively before the heat of the negotiation sways them to accept a poor offer. This sounds prudent, and a bottom line can offer some protection against making a bad deal.

However, a bottom line that looked good before the negotiation may prove unworkable during the negotiation. As offers and counter offers are made, new information comes to light, new interests and currencies are identified, and situations change in various ways, the old bottom line is no longer realistic. By its very nature, a bottom line is rigid; there's no point in having a bottom line that can change!

A bottom line is an arbitrary point. It may have been based on interests as understood at one time, but those interests can change or prove to have been misjudged as the negotiation proceeds. The bottom line figure resembles more of a position than a reflection of interests. Recall that a position is what you think you want, and an interest is what would really serve your needs.

Your bottom line is just a number, or an arbitrary position that may not be meaningful. Your Plan B is a better point of reference. It is a real alternative to a real option on the table. Therefore, you should compare the option before you (a possible solution to the negotiation) with your Plan B (your best alternative solution outside of this negotiation) and decide which one is better for you.

Developing your Plan B

Focus on your key interests and ask yourself how you might satisfy them if you cannot reach an agreement with the other party. List as many alternatives as you can think of. Remember, you are not looking for options — possible solutions to this negotiation — at this time. You are looking for alternatives outside of this negotiation, courses of action you could pursue with other parties or on your own. List the pros and cons for each. Which alternative is most favourable? Is it realistic? If so, this is your Plan B.

ALTERNATIVE	PROS	CONS
1.		
2.		
3.		

Your Plan B is your best alternative at a given point in time. But times change. You can also change your backup plan. You can improve your Plan B or find a new and one. There is no need to cling to your original Plan B throughout the negotiation — you can continue to improve it even as you negotiate. The better your Plan B, the better the agreement you can expect from your negotiating counterpart.

What is their Plan B?

Remember that your counterpart also has a Plan B. You may be able to estimate his Plan B by anticipating his alternatives to dealing with you and identifying the most favourable one. Put yourself in his shoes and try to determine his best alternative.

Just as you may be able to estimate your counterpart's Plan B, he may have some idea what your Plan B is as well. In our earlier example, your boss may know what Other Company and ThirdCo pay their employees.

Diminishing their Plan B

While Plan Bs can be improved, they can also be made to appear less attractive. The idea is to improve your Plan B and suggest that your counterpart's is weaker than he thinks it is. Of course, you need to be subtle and tactful about this. You also need to understand that your counterpart may use this tactic on you. However, if your Plan B is realistic and strong enough, you can resist this.

Returning to our example, suppose your boss says she can only increase your salary to $3,700. What is her best alternative if you resign? She may be able to hire a younger person for less than she was paying you. Her Plan B looks good, perhaps even better than giving you a raise! How can you make it look weaker?

You can suggest that it will be troublesome and expensive to recruit a replacement for you. The new hire will take time before he can get up to speed and be productive. He may not work out at all and your boss will be back at square one, so why take the risk? Now her Plan B doesn't look so good, and she might decide to increase her offer. Alternatively, she might try to diminish your Plan B by suggesting that Other Company are slave drivers, they have a dysfunctional culture, so why leave your friends and a good position for a lousy couple of hundred dollars more?

There are other ways of making a Plan B seem less attractive than by trying to persuade your counterpart that it is so. Suppose you are negotiating to purchase a house. Your offer of $372,000 is a bit less than the seller would like. What is the seller's Plan B? Perhaps another prospect has expressed a willingness to buy the house for $374,500. What can you do to weaken his Plan B? Put down a cash deposit. The other prospect's words may sound sweeter, but they are only words, and money talks. The seller's Plan B suddenly seems less attractive next to your cold, hard cash.

Walking away

Psychologically, it may be difficult to walk away from a negotiation. You have invested time, effort, money and psychic energy, and you don't want all of that to be for nothing. You may feel that your constituents are counting on you to reach an agreement, and they would be disappointed if you came back without one. You may feel pressure from the other party to 'do your part' to make the deal happen. You may even look at your bottom line and decide that it was too unrealistic after all, and accept a proposal you should rule out.

 Aha! Moment

I can walk away if necessary. Negotiation is a voluntary process. No deal at all is better than a bad deal.

Focus on your interests! Remember that whatever resources you have invested are sunk costs and are irrelevant in evaluating whether an agreement makes sense at this time. Your constituents may be expecting an agreement, but after the fog clears they will be more disappointed with a bad one than none at all. The approval of your counterpart is not a valid consideration, so do not feel pressure to conclude an agreement just for his sake. Your bottom line may offer some protection against accepting a bad deal, but it may be too rigid in light of new information and currencies that come up during the course of the negotiation.

Do not use any of these factors to determine whether to conclude an agreement. The only thing to consider is your Plan B. Compare the best option on the table with your Plan B and decide which serves your interests better.

Having a strong Plan B is an indispensable part of preparing for your negotiation. A strong Plan B ensures that you will not settle for less than you can get elsewhere, and gives you confidence that you can reach a more favourable agreement during a negotiation. By improving your Plan B and undermining your counterpart's Plan B, you can expect an even better outcome.

Always have a Plan B.

Star Tips for developing and using your Plan B

1. Prepare thoroughly for every negotiation, but understand there are no guarantees.

2. Always have a backup plan — a Plan B.

3. Decide how you can best satisfy your interests elsewhere if this negotiation does not result in a satisfactory agreement.

4. Formulate your Plan B before every negotiation. Your Plan B gives you confidence and guarantees you will not be worse off by negotiating with this party.

5. Do not bluff. Your Plan B must be realistic.

6. Understand that a rigid bottom line is not as good a standard of comparison as your Plan B.

7. Seek to improve your Plan B or find a better alternative.

8. Find ways to diminish the value of your counterpart's Plan B in his eyes.

9. Compare the best option on the table with your Plan B and decide accordingly.

10. Walk away if necessary. No deal at all is better than a bad deal.

NEGOTIATING POWER

*"Necessity never made
a good bargain."*

Benjamin Franklin

6

People in my negotiation workshops often lament that they feel powerless compared to the people they negotiate with. Perhaps you feel the same way. You shouldn't. In fact, there are all kinds of negotiating power.

Legitimate power

Legitimate power refers to power associated with a position or office. For example, a vice president of a major corporation or the head of a government department has power that comes with her position. Whoever holds the office holds the power, regardless of their intellect, competence or personality.

Legitimate power is often expressed through an impressive title, a magnificent office desk and chair, and a luxuriously appointed conference room. The holder of such power has influence with political big-wigs and corporate titans, instant access to the media, and an army of lackeys to do his bidding. He wears expensive tailored suits, sports a fine Swiss watch, and entertains clients at the most exclusive clubs. It is easy to see how anyone not part of his exalted circle could feel intimidated.

You may not have a fancy title like your negotiating partner, but some titles are just a lot of hot air. Despite your counterpart's senior title, power suit and club membership, you may be dealing with a weak negotiator.

You will be painfully aware of your own deadlines, sales targets, budget constraints and other pressure points. However, you probably don't know what pressures your counterpart is under, and it is unlikely that she will tell you. Everyone has problems, worries and weaknesses, even Donald Trump and Sir Richard Branson.

Most people tend to overestimate their own pressures and weaknesses, while assuming their counterpart has a stronger position than she really does. When you face a seemingly powerful negotiating partner, it's a good idea to remind yourself that she may have problems of her own. Perhaps she is under pressure to conclude a deal with you, and may not have as strong a hand as she is leading you to believe. You must ignore the trappings of power and focus on your interests.

Fast Fact

Traditional sources of power, such as money and position, are less important than they used to be.

Expertise

An expert is a person who possesses extraordinary skill or knowledge in a particular area. In today's complex, highly specialised world, expertise is a more important source of power than a title.

For example, I've had teenagers help me with computer problems. Despite their youth and lack of a title, these youngsters have power over me due to their superior expertise in the field of computers. When they tell me I need a new thingamabob, I get it. When they say it costs X dollars, I pay it.

Expertise is perhaps the most important form of power today, and anyone can develop it. What type of expertise do you have? How can you develop more expertise in that area, or in complementary areas? By increasing your expertise, you increase your negotiating power.

Perhaps your expertise is well-known. If not, you must let the other party know (subtly, of course) that you are an expert. Make sure he is aware of your credentials. Ask questions that show a high level of understanding, use the appropriate jargon, and refer to other experiences where relevant. You may be able to influence the other party and achieve a more favourable outcome if he recognises your expertise.

Projecting expertise is subject to posturing and hype. It would pay to remember this when you find yourself negotiating with a so-called expert. Do not be taken in by the title, smooth talk or cocky demeanor. It could all be an act. In any case, he is only human, and you both stand to gain from the negotiation.

If you truly are dealing with a bona fide expert, do not be intimidated. Experts are not always right, and their opinion is often just that — an opinion. In almost any major lawsuit, each party will engage an expert. These experts will contradict each other on every critical point. They cannot both be right! Don't assume the expert opposite you is right either.

Information

Information is another source of negotiating power. The more you know about your counterpart, the subject of the negotiation, and your respective industries, the more power you have. For example:

- What does your counterpart really need? What are his true interests? What are his psychological and ego needs?

- Who are his constituents or stakeholders? What are their interests?

- Who are his competitors? What competitive pressures is he facing?

- What is his negotiating style? What tactics does he use?

- What is his financial situation? What are his budget constraints?

- Does he have any deadlines or time constraints? What is his business cycle like?

- Are there any relevant trends or changes occurring in his industry?

- Is there anything in his background or track record of interest to you?

It is easier to gather information before you begin bargaining. Once you begin talking with your counterpart you may find him reluctant to disclose much information, and he may be suspicious of your motives. Begin gathering information as soon as you realise you have an interest that you will have to negotiate to satisfy.

Let's say you want to buy a new computer. Most people would simply go to a dealer, look at a few models, and buy one they think would be suitable. They may later find that it does not meet their needs or that they paid too much for it.

A good negotiator would first determine exactly what her needs are. Then she would research various models that could meet those needs. She would then compare prices at different dealers for her top two or three choices. A really good negotiator would even research the dealers to learn about their business practices and negotiating styles.

It is particularly useful to get information about the other party's needs and interests. Understanding the other party and his interests can give you a tremendous advantage. Find out everything you can about your counterpart, his company and his needs.

Note that people have many needs, and not all of them are obvious. Do not overlook psychological or ego needs, which we discussed in Chapter 4.

You can find a lot of valuable information online, in industry directories and in trade journals. Annual reports and other company publications are full of useful information. You might also talk to people who have previously dealt with the person or organisation you will be negotiating with.

 Fast Fact

With all the information available online, it is easier than ever to boost your negotiating power.

You can even talk to other people within your counterpart's organisation. When shopping for that new computer, wouldn't it be useful to speak candidly with a service technician *before* you approach a salesman? Wouldn't the technician give you valuable information about the pros and cons of various models, even competitors' models, that the salesman would not mention while he is selling to you? That technician would be so flattered that you asked for his opinion that he would lay it all out for you!

Information is like gold. Begin gathering information as early as possible.

 Aha! Moment

The fastest and easiest way for me to increase my negotiating power is with information.

Reward and punishment

We negotiate with someone because we believe he is in a position to help us or hurt us. We want him to help us, or to refrain from hurting us, and we negotiate to try to influence that outcome. We are also in a position to help or hurt our counterpart. Therefore, we each have some measure of power to reward or punish the other.

Whether a party will use that power to reward or punish is a matter of perception. So is the more basic question of whether a party has such power, and how much. If you feel they have power, then they do. And if they feel you have power over them, then you do. Do not wield your power like a club. Let them think you have power, and never disabuse them of that notion, whether it is accurate or not. It is better to keep them guessing than to make it clear that you would never harm their interests.

Competition

Competition is another form of negotiating power. If you have ever bid on a government project, you will know how powerful competition can be. The thought that someone else will offer to do the job for less presses you to lower your bid. Since the number of jobs available is relatively scarce and many bidders are competing for them, the government benefits.

Whenever there is competition for what you are offering — whether it's money, products, services or time — others will value it more. Remind your counterpart that he has competition, or that you have other alternatives. Never appear too eager for a deal. Always have a Plan B.

Your Plan B

Your Plan B is a form of competition. It gives you confidence and guarantees that you will end up better off than you were at the beginning of your negotiation. Develop the strongest Plan B you can, and strive to improve it throughout the negotiation. (See Chapter 5 for a more complete discussion of your Plan B.)

Precedent

A court of law will nearly always follow precedent when handing down a judgement. Precedent refers to the practice of following previous outcomes in similar cases. It allows the courts to be consistent, and it allows citizens to predict whether a proposed course of action is likely to have negative consequences. Society benefits from this fairness and predictability.

In law, precedent is binding. In other fields we often act as though it were as well. The same rationale applies. We like and accept precedent because it makes our life easier, and we like doing things the way they've been done before. So it's a good idea to appeal to precedent whenever it serves your interests.

What if following precedent goes against your interests in a particular situation? Then argue against it. Differentiate your case from the others, and show how this distinction warrants different treatment.

For example, suppose you are negotiating with your boss for a salary increase. You could use precedent to show how other employees in the same position with the same experience and performance are earning more than you, so your request is justified. Your boss might try to find a reason why the precedent should not be followed. Perhaps a poor economy or some other factor makes your comparison irrelevant.

Precedent is a powerful justification for getting people to do something. Use that power when you can, and be prepared to fight it when you must.

Commitment

As you prepare for a negotiation, get the commitment of others on your team. Ask for their input and involvement. Get their buy-in. Their support is a source of power.

Commitment from your team means you are all in this together. All share the risk and reward. Knowing your team is with you gives you confidence. You will feel stronger, and your counterpart will notice this. This psychological edge will help you throughout the negotiation.

The advantage isn't just psychological. Your team's input will help you prepare better because you draw on multiple perspectives and strengths. You will benefit as their knowledge and expertise supplement your own.

Investment

People don't like to lose. We don't like to lose money, waste time, or invest effort without gain. It follows that the more we invest in a negotiation — time, money, effort or psychic energy — the more we want to get something in return. This fear of seeing our investment go down the drain may lead us to accept a poor settlement.

The voice of wisdom tells us that it is better to see our investment gone than to make the situation worse by accepting a bad deal. Unfortunately, we don't always heed this voice.

Be mindful of what you and your counterpart invest in a negotiation. Learn to see your investment as sunk costs that are gone regardless of whether you are able to conclude a satisfactory agreement. However, you don't need to educate your counterpart on this point. Let him see his investment as a reason to reach an agreement with you.

Danger Zone

Do not view expenditures of time, effort or money as an investment that must yield a return. It may be an investment that gives you the benefit of knowing that you shouldn't make a deal.

You might even remind your counterpart of his investment. "Gee, it's too bad you can't raise your offer any higher. After all the time we've spent on this, it would be a shame to walk away empty-handed. Are you sure you can't find a bit more money in the budget?"

You can even leverage on your counterpart's investment. Negotiate and agree on the easier issues first. Save the difficult ones for last. In light of his investment, your counterpart may become more accommodating.

Persistence

When you were a toddler you were eager to walk about like everyone else. Imagine if you had quit trying to walk the first time you fell down. You'd still be crawling around the floor today! But you persisted, because you wanted it badly enough.

Most people give up too easily. They try something, they fail, and they quit. They ask for something, get a "no", and they give up. They are afraid to pursue the matter for fear of failing again. They stop asking in case they are seen as overbearing, or because they don't want to risk further rejection.

The word "no" is not carved in stone. It is usually a gut reaction to a proposal that has not been well considered. The same request, in another time and place, might get a "yes". When you hear a "no", treat it as an opening position. Make a counter offer. Modify your request. Explore other possibilities. Be persistent. You may just succeed in turning that "no" into a "yes".

Many successful negotiations begin with the word "no". How they end depends on how persistent you are.

Attitude

The right attitude is a wonderful source of power. And if your attitude is not ideal, you can change it. What is the right attitude for a win-win negotiator? Here are some guidelines:

1. Ask for more than you expect. Negotiators with higher aspirations generally end up with more. Be positive.

2. Approach the negotiation as a problem to be resolved in collaboration with your counterpart. Do not enter a negotiation looking for ways to beat your adversary.

3. Be willing to take calculated risks. The casino does not win every bet, but they always win in the long run.

4. Be persistent. Don't give up or compromise until you have explored all possibilities. Remember that the reason win-win outcomes are so rare is not that it can't be done, but that the win-win solution has not been found.

5. Treat the negotiation as a game. Take the game seriously but not personally. Be objective. Don't get too attached emotionally to the subject of the negotiation. Be prepared to walk away if you can't get what you want on satisfactory terms.

6. Appreciate the power of time. Most progress towards agreement happens towards the end of the negotiation. Try to ascertain your counterpart's time constraints. The party with the least time constraint has an advantage over the one with a tight deadline.

7. Remember that you can walk away if necessary. Negotiation is a voluntary process. No deal is better than a bad deal.

8. Finally, negotiating power is largely a matter of perception. Be prepared, be confident, and project a sense of power. If they *think* you have the power, then you really *do* have the power.

Persuasiveness

The power of persuasion is a boon to any negotiator. You will recall that negotiation is a persuasive process. It is a way of getting others to do what you want them to do. How successful you are at persuading your counterpart depends on three factors:

- **Credibility.** Do you look the part, sound knowledgeable and confident, have relevant experience or expertise, and enjoy a good reputation? Do you represent an organisation that possesses these qualities?

- **Logic.** Do you have facts, evidence, and statistics on your side? Is your reasoning sound? Can you point to specific examples that support your position?

- **Emotion.** Do you speak with passion and conviction? A dynamic and enthusiastic presentation is more persuasive than a dry one. Can you identify your counterpart's hot button?

People decide based on emotion and justify their decisions with reason. Make an emotional appeal to move the other party, but provide him with a logical hook to hang his hat on.

 Aha! Moment

'Logic alone is not enough to persuade others. I need to be credible and passionate as well.

People skills

Having good people skills is a source of power for a win-win negotiator. It's essential to communicate clearly and smoothly. You need to show concern and respect for the other party and value your relationship. You must empathise with him, even when you do not agree.

It also helps to be likeable. Smile, be friendly and approachable, and take a personal interest in your counterpart. Some people truly believe that they can keep warm and fuzzy feelings from influencing them during a hard-nosed business negotiation, but win-win negotiators know better!

We will look more closely at people skills in the next chapter.

Star Tips for using your negotiating power

1. Remind yourself that your seemingly powerful negotiating counterpart has problems and weaknesses of his own.

2. Develop your expertise. Project it to influence negotiating outcomes, and don't be blinded by your counterpart's purported expertise.

3. Gather as much information as you can, and begin doing so as soon as you realise you have an interest that you will have to negotiate to satisfy.

4. Have a strong Plan B. It's a tremendous source of negotiating power.

5. Point to precedent when it supports your position, and question it when it doesn't.

6. Understand the psychological impact of invested time, money and effort.

7. Treat every "no" as a temporary position, and keep trying until you turn it into a "yes".

8. Adopt the right attitude for negotiating — positive, ambitious, open-minded, persistent, and objective.

9. Persuade your counterpart with both logical and emotional appeals.

10. Use solid communication and people skills to win over the other party.

COMMUNICATION AND RELATIONSHIP ISSUES

7

"The most important single ingredient in the formula of success is knowing how to get along with people."

Theodore Roosevelt

The importance of maintaining relationships

There was a time not long ago when business was a jungle. Negotiating was very competitive, a win-lose affair. Businessmen ate each other for lunch. The strong survived, and a killer instinct was prized. That was the norm.

In the old days, railroads swallowed one another whole. Today, airlines form alliances, share codes, and recognise one another's frequent flyer miles. McDonald's sells Coca-Cola in its stores and gives away Disney toys. Computer makers pack their wares with the products of other companies — Intel, Microsoft, Dolby, and so on. These are not casual flings, they are more akin to marriages. Both parties desire long-term benefits.

It isn't just the business world that has become more interdependent. Countries are finding more and more reasons to collaborate. A continent that has historically been plagued with wars has now joined into the European Union. A rising China, formerly mistrusted by the West, is welcomed into the world community.

Times have changed. Sure, there are still plenty of tough guys out there who still follow the laws of the jungle, but their days are numbered. There may also be one-off negotiations where you just want a quick win and don't particularly care how your counterpart fares. No one is holding a gun to his head, and he can choose to make a deal or not. However, these occasions are now the exceptions rather than the rule.

An interdependent world requires collaboration. It demands win-win outcomes. Relationships are important. And at the heart of any relationship is communication.

The window of opportunity

We usually form an impression of someone within four seconds or four minutes of our first contact, depending on which expert you consult. People make a judgement about you based on your appearance, your voice, and elements of non-verbal communication such as your posture and gaze. They will form an impression of you when they first speak with you on the phone or read your first e-mail to them.

Unfair, isn't it? You may not be at your best at your first contact. Your e-mail may have one or two typos. But you will still be judged on this limited and possibly misleading information. The good and the bad all go into the mix, and shape the perceptions that others form of you. While it may not be fair, you can do your best to use it to your advantage rather than let it hurt you. This window of opportunity is narrow so make the most of it.

 Myth Buster

> When e-mailing someone for the first time, I should use very formal language.
>
> On the contrary. Since you are not meeting face-to-face, you cannot offer a hearty handshake, a warm smile of welcome, or show your intense interest with your eyes or posture. While it is not easy, you must try very hard to get something of this in every message you send, particularly when writing to someone new.

This Myth Buster is taken from E-mail Etiquette *by Shirley Taylor, another book in the ST Training Solutions Success Skills Series.*

How can you increase the odds that others will form favourable impressions of you? How can you convey the image you wish to communicate, before you even say "Hello"? How can you project a positive image over the phone or via e-mail with someone you have never met? Here are my suggestions:

1. **Decide on the image you wish to project.** What qualities should a first-rate negotiator possess? No doubt confidence, competence, preparedness and professionalism rank high on that list. Strive to project these qualities.

2. **Make a grand entrance.** Walk tall, with confidence and purpose, like you own the place. You want people to see that you are comfortable in your surroundings. Do not meander aimlessly or look around like you're confused or nervous.

3. **Look like a winner.** Your appearance is critical. Dress better than the average person in your position. Make sure you are well-groomed. Have a nice pen, and keep your documents in an elegant bag or portfolio. This shows you are organised and attentive to detail.

4. **Make the first move.** Don't wait for the other person to make the call; pick up the phone. Introduce yourself or greet her first. People respect those who take the initiative.

5. **Use a firm and friendly handshake.** Make sure your hand is dry, and use a firm grip. Smile warmly and make eye contact. Radiate warmth, sincerity and enthusiasm. Let the other person know you are happy to see him.

6. **Use a confident voice.** You don't want to sound loud and arrogant, nor do you want to speak too softly. Speak in a measured, deliberate and self-assured tone. Avoid fillers and erratic pauses that suggest uncertainty or hesitation. Do not end sentences with an upward inflection that sounds like a question. Use a slower pace as this sounds more authoritative than a faster one. Be calm and in control.

7. **Have an opening line ready.** Know what you want to say, then say it clearly and confidently. Do not fumble over your words — it makes you sound unsure of yourself and your ideas sound half-baked.

8. **Be professional.** Keep your promises, arrive for appointments on time, and follow up on tasks. Treat others with courtesy and respect, whether they are the CEO, the receptionist, or the janitor. Be honest and maintain your integrity.

 Fast Fact

First impressions are formed quickly and set the tone for the relationship that follows.

The halo effect

First impressions are necessarily based on limited and imperfect information. This does not mean they are tentative or easily changed. We tend to generalise and stereotype a person's characteristics based on whatever information we have available. When we see certain favourable qualities in a person, we often assume they also possess other favourable qualities even though there may be no basis for doing so. This tendency is called 'the halo effect'.

Studies have shown that teachers often assume that more attractive students are also more intelligent, and evaluate them accordingly. Those with more appealing names also receive preferential treatment. Businessmen who look like a million bucks get more upgrades on airlines and at hotels than their casually dressed colleagues. It may not be fair but it happens all the time, so we ought to make the most of it!

 Fast Fact

If you increase the number of favourable qualities you project, you will also increase the probability that others will form a more positive impression of you.

You cannot control the impressions others will have of you, but you can influence them. Do what you can with the factors that are easiest to control, such as your clothing, grooming, accessories, behaviour, voice, and other non-verbal communication. Project confidence, competence, preparedness, and professionalism. Let these bright spots create a shiny halo that allows others to see you in the best light.

Aha! Moment

I can leverage my best qualities to enhance the way people perceive me in other areas as well.

Myth Buster

If the person you are dealing with does not have a positive impression of you, you are doomed.

Not necessarily, but you have some remedial work to do. First mpressions easily become lasting impressions and resist change, but there is hope.

Most people pretend there is nothing wrong, even when something clearly is. Address the problem directly. Apologise if warranted, and explain if you think it will help. Take responsibility. Everyone makes mistakes or has an off day, and most people are willing to let you make amends. Work hard to win back their trust and confidence.

Communicate clearly

Use simple language to reduce the risk of misunderstandings. Do not try to impress with big words when common, everyday words will do. Do not use slang, abbreviations, or jargon that your counterpart may not understand. When in doubt, decide in favour of simplicity. Ask to make sure, but be careful not to ask in a condescending tone.

Speak clearly, and enunciate well. If you speak quickly, slow your pace down to match your counterpart's. If you have reason to believe your counterpart might not understand your accent or pronunciation, ask him to let you know if he is unsure about anything you may say. Many people feel awkward asking someone they don't understand to repeat what they said, or to speak more slowly, or to spell a word. Be proactive about avoiding miscommunication.

Be familiar with the jargon of your industry as well as your counterpart's industry. You may not understand 'corporatese' or 'legalese' or 'computerese'. If you do not understand a term or expression, ask for clarification. Never pretend you understand something when you don't. You just may end up agreeing to something you don't want!

Even when not using jargon, do not assume you understand what your counterpart is saying. Paraphrase his statements and ask questions to clarify meaning.

Show respect

Treat your counterpart with respect. Listen to her without interruption. Do not use an arrogant or condescending tone when speaking to her. Thank her for her time and input, and recognise any contributions that she makes.

You can also show respect by being polite and courteous. People like to hear "please" and "thank you." Invite your counterpart to precede you through the door. If you are the host, offer your guest coffee, tea, or other refreshment. Try to anticipate her needs and be accommodating. If you are the guest, make an appreciative comment about your host or his office. You want to be seen as pleasant and likeable in your counterpart's eyes.

If your counterpart is from another country or culture, learn something about his values and customs. Ask questions that show a sincere interest and desire to learn about him as an individual. This shows you value him as a person and will help to put him at ease. As a result, communication will flow better, and intentions are less likely to be misinterpreted.

Create rapport

Rapport means putting another person at ease and making a real connection. You must aim for this right from the beginning. Be polite, friendly, and welcoming. Make small talk. Use the person's name. Smile. Offer him a drink or do him a small favour. Set a friendly tone and establish a collaborative working dynamic.

The essence of rapport is similarity and harmony. When two people are truly in rapport, their tone, pace, rhythm, volume and many elements of their body language will be similar. This will occur naturally, though you can encourage the process by consciously mirroring elements of your counterpart's vocal quality and body language. Position yourself at his level — sit if he is sitting, and stand if he is standing. Use body language beyond the basic eye contact, smile and handshake to create a feeling of similarity.

You can also emphasise similarity and encourage rapport by adopting similar vocabulary as the other party. If she tends to use certain expressions, use them yourself. She will notice, perhaps subconsciously, that there is something about you that she likes. People like people who are like themselves, so you want to be like the person you are with.

Empathise

The renowned psychologist Carl Rogers described empathy as non-judgementally entering another person's world. When you enter his world openly and see it as he sees it, you can truly understand him. You don't need to agree with him, just try to understand his point of view.

Lawyers have a saying that an agreement is a meeting of the minds. In other words, if you and I both have the same idea in mind then we are in agreement. Imagine if we could not only have a meeting of the minds but a meeting of the hearts as well. If you could understand what I am thinking and also feel what I am feeling — that's empathy!

Ask questions

Asking questions allows you to build rapport, gather information, confirm understanding, and control the pace and direction of the negotiation. Ask a lot of questions, and listen to the answers.

Listen

Let your counterpart do most of the talking. The more he talks, the more information you learn. You already know what you think — wouldn't it be great to know what your counterpart thinks? Listening also shows that you respect him and that you are interested in his views.

Pay attention to non-verbal communication

Non-verbal communication is often more important than words alone. Is your counterpart open and approachable, or defensive and secretive? Is he honest, or deceptive? Is he interested, eager, desperate, confused? Learn to read the body language and facial expressions of your counterpart.

Non-verbal communication is a two-way street. Be aware of the non-verbal signals you are sending to others. Drumming your fingers on the table might suggest you are nervous or impatient. Arms crossed across your chest can signal that you are defensive or uncomfortable. Lack of eye contact suggests lack of confidence. Avoid body language and facial expressions that convey weak or negative qualities. Use body language that suggests the qualities you want to project: confidence, competence, preparedness and professionalism. Remember to keep your halo polished and gleaming.

Try This

Ask a few close friends to candidly assess you on mannerisms through which you may be unwittingly sending out the wrong signals. Work on improving in those areas.

Substantive and personality issues

In every negotiation there are substantive issues and personality issues. Substantive issues concern the subject of the negotiation. For example, issues such as price, quantity, delivery dates, payment schedules, and other terms and conditions are substantive issues. We bargain over these issues as we strive to reach a win-win agreement.

There are also personality issues that enter any negotiation and affect the parties' relationship. Your counterpart may have certain habits and mannerisms that irritate you. Perhaps he is loud, insensitive and intimidating. He may always arrive late, talk excessively, and keep you longer than expected. He may try to pressure you with hardball tactics or rush you into making a hasty decision. Or she may be very charming and try to sweet talk you into conceding more than you had planned. Here are my suggestions for dealing with substantive and personality issues:

- **Keep personality issues separate from substantive ones**

    It is easy to let our like or dislike of our counterpart influence the way we deal with him. If we like him, we may allow him more generous terms than we might otherwise. If we don't like him, we may let our feelings distract us from our interests. If we are intimidated by him, we may make concessions on some issues in the hope of winning his approval.

Separate the people from the problem. Do not let personality factors influence you. When a charming counterpart asks you for a concession, ask yourself whether you would make this concession to someone you don't like. Your response should be the same. Do not make concessions on substantive issues in exchange for concessions on personality. Negotiate on the issues, focus on your interests, and look at the big picture.

- **Say no to the request, not to the person**

  Bear in mind that people do not always distinguish the messenger from the message. Even though you may not intend your refusal to be a personal rejection, some people will take it that way. Help them maintain perspective by being clear that you are rejecting the request and not the person making it. For example, say "I cannot agree to that condition" rather than "I cannot help you with that."

- **Give reasons, not excuses**

  When rejecting a proposal, first say what you like about it. Look for common ground, a point of agreement. Then explain what you do not like about it, or what you would change, and why. People like to know why. Explaining your reasoning helps the other party to understand.

- **Avoid negative words and characterisations**

  Strong negative words are highly charged. Their impact can spread from the problem to the people. For example, using strong negative language to refer to a proposal may be taken personally by the speaker. Your characterisation of their idea is taken as a personal slight or insult. In addition, using negative words will colour you as a negative or unlikeable person in the eyes of your audience.

Danger Zone

It is easy to allow personal feelings to affect business relationships. However, do not make concessions on substantive matters to buy approval or make the relationship smoother.

Develop trust

The foundation of any good negotiating relationship is trust. Negotiators who have a trusting relationship are able to reach better agreements in less time and with less formality. They are less likely to have disputes, and are more likely to resolve the disputes amicably when they do arise.

You can build a trusting relationship by getting to know your counterpart as an individual. Spend time socialising and getting to know one another informally. In some cultures this getting acquainted process is critical, and they won't get down to business until they feel comfortable with their counterpart.

Getting to know one another socially is not enough. You must also be trust*worthy*. You must earn and deserve another person's trust. Here are some ways to develop your trustworthiness:

• **Be honest.** Keep your word and maintain a reputation for truthfulness.

• **Be transparent.** Being open and above board will allow others to trust you. You don't have to tell them everything; it is perfectly acceptable to tell your counterpart that certain information is confidential.

- **Be consistent.** People are more comfortable with those who have a clear set of values and follow them without fail. Always under-promise and over-deliver.

- **Value the relationship.** In an ongoing relationship with a valued partner, the future of the relationship is more important than the outcome of any single negotiation. Make sure your counterpart knows you feel this way.

- **Be trusting.** Trust is a two-way street. If you want people to trust you, you have to show you trust them. You need not trust them blindly of course, but be willing to take calculated risks.

 Myth Buster

There's no point in negotiating when there is no trust.

That's not true. Even though you may not trust your counterpart, you can still negotiate fruitfully if you trust the process. Nations often negotiate with one another even when there is low trust because they trust the institutional framework of the international community. Similarly, your bank won't allow a lack of trust to stop them from giving you a loan. They have faith in the banking system and the legal system.

Sharing information

Negotiators talk and listen to one another, but they do not share much information. No doubt this is because information is power, and we want to have more power than the other party. However, hoarding information and treating every bit of data like it's top secret is counterproductive.

Myth Buster

It is dangerous to reveal one's true interests to the other party.

Wrong! A win-win negotiator knows that it is important to identify interests. Sharing information about interests helps the parties reach a win-win agreement. If you alone know your interests, you might be able to satisfy them. But if your counterpart knows your interests as well, she might think of a solution that satisfies your interests that you overlooked. As the old saying goes, two heads are better than one.

Sharing information about interests and other areas increases the likelihood of a win-win. It also encourages trust. After all, it's hard to trust someone who acts secretively. If you share information, your counterpart is likely to reciprocate. You both benefit.

What if the other party does not reciprocate by sharing information with you? You still benefit. As long as your interests are clearly made known, it is more likely that they will be satisfied.

 Fast Fact

Sharing information does have its limits. You may not want to share information about your bottom line, your Plan B, deadlines, or trade secrets. But most people are far more guarded about disclosing information than they should be. Let the information flow more freely and I think you'll find you will achieve more win-win agreements.

Star Tips for improving your communication and relationships

1. Make a strong first impression by projecting confidence, competence, preparedness and professionalism.

2. Use the halo effect to your advantage.

3. Communicate clearly to reduce the risk of misunderstandings.

4. Treat your counterpart with respect. Be courteous and polite.

5. Show interest in your counterpart by getting to know him as an individual.

6. Pay attention to non-verbal communication — both the other party's and your own.

7. Separate personality issues from substantive ones.

8. Avoid negative words and characterisations that could harm the relationship.

9. Build trust to keep the relationship strong.

10. Share information about interests to increase the likelihood of a win-win agreement.

EMOTIONS IN NEGOTIATION

"What makes humanity is not reason. Our emotions are what make us human."

E.O. Wilson

The role of emotion in negotiation

Emotions are always present in every human activity, including negotiation. We all have them, so we have to live with them — ours and theirs. We cannot ignore them, because they affect us all. Emotions affect the way we think, feel and act. The best thing to do is recognise them and deal with them constructively.

Some emotions are positive: joy, confidence, fun. Others are negative: anger, fear, embarrassment. Negative emotions tend to stimulate competitive impulses, which lead to a win-lose dynamic. Positive emotions encourage co-operation and support win-win outcomes.

Emotions are also contagious. We can spread them to, and catch them from, others. Generally, the person who expresses her emotions more forcefully will influence the one who is less expressive.

The implications for negotiation are straightforward. A win-win negotiator will manage the negative emotions in herself and not provoke them in others. She will also display positive emotions, and will say and do things that are likely to bring out positive emotions in others. Sounds simple enough, doesn't it? Unfortunately, it's not simple — not even for Freud!

 Aha! Moment

I cannot avoid my emotions, but I can manage them.

The language of emotion

Many people think of negotiation as a competition. Win-win negotiators think of it as an opportunity to collaborate and solve a common problem together. The language you use can support or detract from these mindsets, so that's why it's important to choose your words wisely.

EMOTIONS IN NEGOTIATION   127

Words such as '*I*', '*me*', '*my*', '*mine*', '*you*', '*your*', and '*yours*' support a competitive negotiating dynamic. '*I*' and '*you*' contrast sharply and make it clear that we are at opposite ends of the spectrum. These words suggest that I will win and you will lose, or you will win and I will lose. It is difficult to reach a win-win outcome with a '*me against you*' mentality.

There may be times when you need to say '*I*' or '*you*', but try to avoid these words whenever possible. Instead, try to use '*we*', '*us*', and '*our*'. These words express collaboration and suggest we are both on the same side, working together to solve our problem.

Using '*we*' and other collaborative language helps set the tone for a win-win. However, when it does come down to '*I*' or '*you*', an '*I*' statement works better than a '*you*'. For example:

"*Your asking price is too high.*"

This sounds judgemental, with an opinion dressed as fact. There is also an implied criticism, which will put the other party on the defensive. He may respond by holding onto his position more tightly and trying to justify it in a confrontational dynamic. Consider this instead:

"*I feel that your asking price is too high.*"

This is my opinion. It is how I feel. We are all entitled to our own feelings and opinions. If I can offer a reason in support it is even better. In any event it is non-judgemental and non-confrontational. We can carry on negotiating without any bad feelings.

In addition to using '*I*' rather than '*you*', these examples emphasise feelings and perceptions. Your counterpart may not share your feelings or perceptions, but he can hardly fault you for them. Here are some more guidelines to remember:

- Avoid using words that suggest the other party is to blame or is wrong. Do not criticise, judge or find fault. This will only put your counterpart on the defensive. Instead, emphasise your feelings and perceptions. For example, consider:

  "Don't rush me!"

  This suggests that the other party is unfairly pressuring me. It suggests I am judging him. He may resent the implication.

  "I'd like some time to think about it."

  This expresses my feelings without regard to the other party's motives. It cannot cause offence.

- Describe rather than judge. An objective description of fact may be disputed, but its mere form will not offend the way a judgement will. For example:

  "Your offer is unreasonably low."

  Your counterpart may be offended by this judgement on your part. You are saying he is unreasonable.

  "I feel your offer of a three per cent increase is inadequate in light of current industry trends."

  This statement is more specific, descriptive, and verifiable, even if "current industry trends" is debatable. It is non-judgemental and unlikely to cause offence.

- The words we use in a negotiation greatly affect its emotional climate. Avoid negative words, value-laden words and emotional or hot button words. Use positive, collaborative and constructive words.

Common emotions in negotiation

Humans experience many feelings and emotions, most of which have little impact on a negotiation. The two that are most likely to derail a negotiation are anger and fear.

Anger

Anger is widely thought to be an ugly emotion, a monster that pops out in stressful situations to urge us on to intimidate, punish and extract revenge. Anger is the most difficult emotion to control. While it may seem appropriate to display anger at the time, in retrospect it rarely is, and we usually regret it afterwards. However, there is another way to look at anger. It serves to protect us against some perceived threat to our well-being or self-esteem.

We also express anger in an attempt to cause the other party to feel fear, thereby giving us some control over them. This is easy to understand when we are focused on winning, getting our way, or proving ourselves to be 'right'. We must appear strong and in control. Anger lets us do this.

As anger is a protective emotion, when we feel anger we must ask what we are protecting ourselves against. We perceive a threat. What is the threat? Similarly, when we see another person expressing anger we must remember that he feels threatened. What is he threatened by? What is he trying to protect?

Myth Buster

Anger is a sign of strength.

On the contrary. Anger is often a sign of weakness or vulnerability being protected. True strength consists of controlling our anger and channeling it in an appropriate manner. While it may be natural to feel anger, a win-win negotiator will react to it constructively. Unless anger is managed it can derail a negotiation, and a relationship.

The rule is: don't express your anger. Of course, there are exceptions. If you do express anger, do so because you *choose to act angry* when justified. For example, a hard-nosed negotiator may provoke you to test your response. While remaining calm and in control is normally the best response, you may decide that a controlled release of anger or a display of righteous indignation will show your counterpart that you are not a pushover. Mr Tough Guy might interpret this as a show of strength and respect you more for it. Having proved your mettle, he won't mess with you again.

Some negotiators will unleash an outburst of anger in the hope of extracting a concession from you. However, win-win negotiators are able to create value without stooping to such low tactics.

Suppose your counterpart is not a win-win negotiator. Suppose he cannot control his emotions, or uses his anger as a club. How should you respond? Here are my suggestions:

• First of all, you must allow his anger to run its course. You cannot reason with someone in an emotionally charged state, so don't even try. Stop the discussion. Let him vent. This would be a good time to take a break. Resume negotiating only after his anger has dissipated.

- Just because a person has calmed down, do not assume he is no longer angry. Chances are the feelings underlying the anger are still there. You must address these concerns, but only after the emotional storm has passed.

- Accept his anger as valid. While expressing anger is not always appropriate, your counterpart has a right to his feelings. Empathise. You might say:

    "I see you are angry. You obviously feel strongly about this, and I'd like to understand why this is so important to you."

Encourage him to share his thoughts, and listen attentively.

- Maintain your own composure in the face of an angry outburst from your counterpart. Do not fight fire with fire — you'll only get a bigger fire!

- Do not take it personally. Your counterpart may be angry with himself, frustrated with the situation, or trying to mask his own weakness or insecurity. Do not assume you are the target, because chances are you are not.

- Do not appease your counterpart by offering a concession. Make a concession only in exchange for a concession from your counterpart, and only at a point when reason prevails. Once you give something up to buy approval from the other party, guess what you'll get? More outbursts! And why not — your counterpart will have discovered a successful strategy for negotiating with you.

- Apologise when warranted, or even when it's not. An apology costs nothing, and it makes the other party feel better. Don't let pride stand in the way of satisfying your interests. Focus on the big picture.

 Aha! Moment

I am not negotiating to prove that I am right or to serve my ego; I am negotiating to satisfy my interests.

Fear

There are four basic types of fear: fear of the unknown, fear of loss, fear of failure, and fear of rejection. They all have implications for negotiators, so you should understand how they affect you and your counterpart and be prepared to deal with them.

Fear of the unknown

People fear what they do not know or understand. A negotiation may have high stakes and an uncertain outcome; even the process may be unknown and inspire fear.

The antidote to this is preparation. Learn as much as you can about your interests and currencies, as well as those of your counterpart. Develop a strong Plan B. Gather information about the subject matter and context of the negotiation. Preparation leads to confidence, and confidence helps you manage fear.

Fear of loss

No one likes to lose, but some people have a strong aversion to risk. In fact, most people are more strongly motivated by a fear of loss than they are by the prospect of gain. Their fear of losing money or paying too much can cause them to miss out on a good opportunity. Conversely, their fear of missing out on an opportunity can cause them to make a bad deal.

Preparation also helps combat fear of loss. Before you begin bargaining, know your bottom line and your Plan B, and stick to them. Be prepared to walk away. You may reassess these in light of new information and changing situations, but do so with the same sobriety as went into your initial pre-negotiation assessment.

In addition, understand that a calculated risk is not the same as a foolish risk. There is always some element of risk in a negotiation. However, if you allow yourself to become paralysed with fear, you will not negotiate much, nor will you gain much. Remember that negotiation has elements of skill and chance, and the more skillful you are at preparing the less you will be affected by chance.

Fear of failure

While fear of loss and fear of failure often go together, fear of loss relates to tangibles (money, opportunity) while fear of failure relates to intangible losses, such as damage to pride, ego, or reputation, or embarrassment or loss of face. These emotional losses may be harder to bear than monetary losses.

The very prospect of losing face can cause a negotiator to ignore his best interests and embrace a losing cause. Because he doesn't want to admit he was wrong, he continues to pursue a doomed strategy in the irrational hope that things will turn out well. This escalation of commitment strikes even seasoned negotiators. Guard against it with thorough pre-negotiation preparation and by asking team members for reality checks during the negotiation.

A win-win mindset can offset fear of failure, as well as fear of losing and fear of the unknown. Approaching a negotiation as a chance to solve a problem collaboratively with your counterpart minimises fear of failing or losing, as the focus is on getting a win for both parties. The emphasis on asking questions, listening and empathising builds trust and sheds light on the unknown. The spirit of exploring options and creating value keeps the discussion positive as fear takes a back seat.

Fear of rejection

A special fear of failure is fear of rejection. We don't like to hear the word "no." Most people, upon hearing the word "no," get discouraged and give up. They equate rejection of their request as a rejection of them personally. They are afraid to pursue the matter for fear they may be seen as overbearing. Sometimes they just don't want to risk further rejection.

To overcome this fear of rejection, remind yourself that only your idea is being rejected, perhaps because your counterpart doesn't understand your request. Follow up with a "why not?" to understand her thinking. Make sure she understood you.

The word "no" is rarely final. Whenever you hear a "no," treat it as an opening position. Modify your proposal and consider other options. Try to turn that "no" into a "yes."

The key to overcoming these fears is preparation — a major theme that I've been emphasising throughout this book. In addition, remember these tips:

- Do not appear too eager for a deal. Once you demonstrate an emotional desire for the subject of the negotiation, your counterpart will be able to deal with you on his terms.

- Have a strong Plan B. This gives you confidence and guarantees you will not be worse off after the negotiation than you were before.

- Be prepared to walk away. Making a bad deal is worse than making no deal at all.

 Danger Zone

Do not show fear. Wear your poker face. Remember that much of negotiating power is based on perception. It's important to appear confident and in control.

Bear in mind that your negotiating counterpart, being human, also experiences these fears to some degree. How much will depend on his perceptions, level of confidence, preparation, and strength of will.

Managing expectations — keeping them happy

In Chapter 3 we looked at a situation in which your neighbour offered an antique cabinet at his yard sale for $200, and you accepted his offer immediately. He got his asking price, but the speed of your acceptance and the look of glee on your face gave him second thoughts. He expected a bit of haggling, but you didn't play the game. He has an uneasy feeling that he's been had.

Perception is a big part of negotiating. It isn't whether you win or lose that matters, it's whether you *feel* you've won or lost. The subjective outcome is more important than any objective measure of the outcome. People need to feel good about the process and the outcome, regardless of how well they actually fare.

As such, we saw that it is better to haggle and feign reluctance than to accept a first offer. We have to play the game. We have to meet expectations.

In addition, the negotiation process must appear to be fair. People have a powerfully strong sense of fairness — it's hard-wired into our brains. If you or the process seems unfair, your counterpart will resent you and your relationship will suffer.

An activity common in negotiation classes illustrates the point. Students are paired up, and one student is given $100 to share with his partner at his discretion. However, his partner has the right to accept the offer and share the money, or reject it, in which case no one gets any money. A 50:50 offer is invariably accepted. Often the first student will feel entitled to a larger share and offer a 60:40 split, or a 75:25 split. Some of these will be accepted, but the more unequal the proposed split, the more likely the second student will play the spoiler and reject the offer. A rational person would accept an offer of even $1, as he would be better off monetarily. But people aren't rational — they are emotional, and they have a strong sense of fairness. They may choose a lose-lose outcome rather than stand for what they perceive to be unfair treatment.

Aha! Moment

Life is not fair, but people can choose to be fair.

Fast Fact

Win-win negotiators understand how emotional and irrational people can be when they feel they are not being treated fairly. They also know that people demand respect. Consequently, they take pains to be fair and show respect throughout the negotiation. They also make sure the negotiation process itself is fair and impartial.

Biases

We tend to have certain biases in the way we apportion credit and blame. When things turn out favourably for us we are likely to attribute the results to our own ability. "I achieved a good result because I worked hard, I prepared, I am a great negotiator, I deserve it." When we don't do so well we find external reasons to explain the result. "They got lucky, they deceived me, the economy worked against me, there was nothing I could do about it." In the alternative, we may discount the effects of situational factors and assume our counterpart has more skill, expertise or ability than he really does.

A win-win negotiator tries to be objective and open to possibilities. She will still be biased, but she will be more willing to accept that she has faults and makes mistakes. When you take responsibility for your shortcomings, you have an opportunity to learn from your mistakes and do better next time.

We also tend to think things will turn out better for us than for others. "That could never happen to me; it only happens to other people." Then again, some people think they always get the lemons in life, and everyone else has it better.

We also think more highly of ourselves than of others. "I am smarter, more skillful, more honest, more open minded, and fairer than him. He is so rigid, irrational, and biased." Your counterpart probably thinks the same about you!

A win-win negotiator recognises that she and her counterpart both have these biases. She strives to accept the other party as an equal. She understands that by thinking ill of her counterpart their trust and communication will suffer, as will the likelihood of reaching a win-win outcome.

Star Tips for managing emotions while negotiating

1. Display positive emotions and manage negative emotions.

2. Think and speak in collaborative terms of 'we' and 'us' rather than adversarial terms of 'me' and 'you'.

3. Speak in terms of feelings and opinions rather than judgements.

4. Do not attempt to reason with an angry counterpart. Wait until the emotion subsides.

5. Accept your counterpart's anger as a valid emotion, but do not take it personally.

6. Combat fear by being prepared.

7. Treat a "no" as an opening position rather than a final answer. Explore other options that may ultimately result in an agreement.

8. Maintain objectivity and get periodic reality checks to avoid escalating commitment to a losing course of action.

9. Ensure that the negotiation process is perceived as fair by both parties.

10. Understand the effects of biases and compensate for them.

WRAPPING UP: IMPLEMENTATION AND POST-NEGOTIATION MATTERS

9

*"It ain't over
'til it's over."*

Yogi Berra

You've done your homework, asked questions and gathered information, identified interests and currencies, developed a Plan B, created value and options, and finally reached a win-win agreement with your counterpart. You shake hands and congratulate one another on a job well done. Now what?

You feel relieved — exhilarated even. You look forward to enjoying the fruits of your efforts. Perhaps you feel so good that you don't even think about how those fruits will end up on your table.

Shaking hands over your agreement is not the end of the negotiation. Agreements don't implement themselves. There is still more to do!

Memoranda and draft agreements

It's important to take careful notes throughout the negotiation. Whether you are meeting face-to-face or negotiating over the phone, take notes. You'd be surprised how often you and your counterpart forget things, or have different recollections of what was discussed. Your notes will come to the rescue. You may even find that what you and the other party actually agreed to is more favourable to you than what you recalled.

People forget things. Even with the best of intentions, we cannot remember everything. Taking notes makes you more attentive to the negotiation, which is reason enough for taking notes. But taking notes is also a good idea to protect yourself at every stage of the process. If the negotiation is complicated or takes place over a long period of time, draft a memorandum from your notes periodically to reflect the current state of affairs. In any event, you will certainly want a final memorandum at the end of the negotiation. This memorandum may even be the basis for what will become a formal written agreement.

I suggest you should draft any written contract yourself. Your counterpart may genuinely appreciate your taking on this responsibility. But that is not the main reason for doing it. You and your counterpart will inevitably have different understandings about what you are agreeing to, and you will prefer to make your understanding the basis of the final agreement. As you draft the contract, you will naturally shape it according to your understanding. This does not mean you have devious motives; you probably won't even be aware of it. Chances are your counterpart won't be aware of it either.

Try This

Some negotiators like to draft an agreement before they even begin negotiating! This may sound premature, but the idea has merit. It forces you to think about what you really want to get out of the negotiation. It also gives you a chance to set high aspirations. While the final agreement will probably look different than what you earlier conceived, your first draft gives you something to measure the final agreement against. Compare the proposed final agreement with this earlier draft before you finalise it to make sure you didn't overlook anything important.

Your counterpart may also wish to write the contract. If so, read it over carefully. Make sure it conforms to your understanding as reflected in your notes. If anything seems amiss, raise the issue with the other party immediately.

As you haggle over the final terms you may have a series of revisions to make or approve. Do not focus only on the red pencilled changes when comparing drafts. Check all subsequent revisions as carefully as the first draft.

Lawyers spend an inordinate amount of time and charge hefty fees for poring over contracts. It is often worth the extra time and expense.

Implementing the agreement

Have you ever made plans to meet a friend, only to find that the meeting never takes place?

> *"Where were you? You were supposed to meet me last night!"*

> *"No, we discussed it, but you never called back to confirm it."*

> *"But I thought we had agreed to meet. I didn't think we needed to reconfirm."*

It seemed like a simple enough plan at the time, but the two of you had different understandings.

 Fast Fact

Agreements don't implement themselves. People implement agreements. And people sometimes misunderstand, forget, or fail to follow through.

Any written contract should make clear the 'who', 'what', 'when', 'where', and 'how' of the agreement. If there is only an oral agreement, your notes or memos should reflect the parties' understanding. Follow up to make sure both parties are doing what they agreed to do.

Remember the two sisters who squabbled over the orange? They eventually discovered that one wanted to squeeze out the juice, while the other wanted to grate the rind to make a cake. The solution sounds simple enough in theory, but it may not be so simple to execute. Will the thirsty one squeeze out the juice first, and give her sister a messy peel afterwards? Or will the baker grate the rind first, and give her sister a nearly naked and hard to squeeze fruit? When do they each plan on using the parts they need? While they may think their problem was solved, their troubles may not be over yet!

I mentioned earlier that it is wise to draft an agreement before you begin negotiating. At the very least, ask yourself: what will the final agreement look like? Continue to think about this over the course of the negotiations. Ask yourself:

- What steps must be taken? By whom? By when?

- What possible obstacles might arise? Potential misunderstandings? How might you avoid them?

- How can you help your counterpart 'sell' the agreement to his constituents?

- How will the agreement be monitored?

At the end of the formal negotiation, after the final handshake, you will want to celebrate and stop thinking about all the details of the agreement. As time goes by, these details become a blur. You move on to other projects. You assume the deal will happen as planned.

To avoid problems later, make sure the final agreement provides detailed answers to the questions above. At the very least, assign the follow-up work to a particular person who will be held accountable, such as your personal assistant. Provide a clear framework for implementing the agreement.

Nibbles

A nibble is a last-minute attempt by one party to grab an extra concession from his counterpart. For example, a car buyer might ask the salesman to throw in a set of new floor mats, or a home buyer might ask the seller to include certain appliances not already included in the contract.

A nibble is a consciously-employed tactic, not the afterthought it seems to be. The nibbler knows the other party may be feeling generous while basking in the afterglow of a successful negotiation, and he tries to take advantage of this goodwill. Or perhaps the party being nibbled may fear the deal will fall through if he doesn't agree to this relatively minor request. Not wishing to appear petty, he agrees.

A nibble is especially effective after the other party has invested substantial time, effort or mental energy in the negotiation. However, your counterpart will probably resent it. She may feel that you are greedy or you are not negotiating in good faith.

Like all tactics, there is also a counter-tactic to the nibble. In fact, there are several. Let's look at them here:

- First, you might make it contingent. A nibble is a request for a concession, and we do not like to make unilateral concessions. Defend against the nibble by saying, "I might be able to give you that, if you can give me this."

- You can defer to higher authority. "I'd love to give you those floor mats, but my manager would never agree to it."

- If you are in a business where you get the same kind of nibble all the time, put a price on it. "Let's see, according to our standard price list, I can give you that set of new floor mats for only $189. Shall I add that to the purchase order?" People can say anything, but a written price list is the type of authority people don't usually argue with.

- You can appeal to fairness. "Come on now, I've already given you such a good deal. I really can't give any more."

- You can let the nibbler know you're onto his game. "Hey, that was a pretty good nibble!" The nibble is designed to seem casual and not look like a tactic. The tactic doesn't work when the veil is stripped off. Be very careful with this — you don't want to cause the nibbler to lose face when exposing him. Unless you know the person well, consider using one of the other four defences above.

Post-settlement settlements

A post-settlement settlement (PSS) is a settlement that is agreed to after the parties reach their initial agreement. It is not a second, unrelated agreement, but rather an improved version of the first agreement. It allows you to leverage on your success and do even better.

Myth Buster

A post-settlement settlement sounds like an oxymoron. Why would you want to settle an agreement that has already been settled?

The very idea sounds suspect, which may be why these devices are so rarely used. However, a PSS can be a great way to improve an already good deal.

Your initial agreement may not be as good as it could have been. You didn't know the other party that well, and may not have built enough trust to share information as fully as you could have. You may not have thought of all currencies or addressed all interests. You may have accepted a good deal too quickly for fear of losing it, rather than holding out for a better deal. After the dust settles, you think of ways you could have done better. Or maybe you can't think of any particular improvements you would like to make, but you would like to explore further possibilities.

A PSS can create additional value for both parties. The fact that you have reached an agreement shows that you can work with your counterpart. You have built up trust and goodwill, and you have helped one another become better off than you were before you reached your agreement. You both took risks in negotiating, and those risks paid off. With this track record of success in joint problem solving, you are both confident that you can continue to help one another do even better.

A PSS assumes that the initial agreement will remain in effect if the parties are unable to reach a better agreement. You can continue to negotiate with your initial agreement serving as your new Plan B. It is also your counterpart's Plan B. Both of you must do better (or at least be no worse off) than your initial agreement provides or you will not agree to change it.

Aha! Moment

> I have nothing to lose by considering a post-settlement settlement. Either we're both better off, or we abide by our original agreement.

For example, suppose you negotiate an employment package with a new employer. Your agreement states that you will begin your employment in 30 days, which allows you to give the requisite notice to your current employer. Your current employer unexpectedly agrees to waive that requirement and lets you go at the end of the week. The prospect of sitting home without pay for the next three and a half weeks does not excite you, so you call your new employer and ask to re-examine the timing issue. If she would like you to begin immediately, you both are better off. Otherwise, you both stick to your original agreement.

You might be reluctant to raise the idea of a PSS because of what your counterpart might think. He might think you are having second thoughts about the agreement and are trying to back out or extract more concessions from him. He might wonder why you think you could reach a better agreement now — were you not negotiating in good faith earlier? Did you learn something new? Did your situation change? These thoughts do not inspire confidence that your agreement will work out as expected.

It is natural for someone not familiar with the PSS concept to have these doubts. You need to anticipate and overcome them. Emphasise that you are happy with your agreement and intend to honour it. Explain that there might be ways to improve it, and that you would like to explore some ways if they are mutually advantageous. Ask whether your counterpart has similar thoughts, or is at least open to the possibility of improving the agreement.

The fact that the initial agreement — the new Plan B for both parties — guarantees that neither party will be worse off if there is no PSS should make you and your counterpart comfortable in exploring new and better possibilities.

When things get ugly

There will be times when you and your counterpart fail to reach an agreement where failure is not an option (for example, a management-labour negotiation), or you disagree about a provision of an agreement you made earlier. In times like these, one party may break off the negotiations with the words, "I'll see you in court!"

Aside from extreme measures such as war, strikes and lockouts, there are three methods for resolving breakdowns in negotiations: litigation, mediation and arbitration.

Litigation

Glamourised in movies and on TV, litigation is the most familiar means of resolving a dispute. The idea is simple: the parties go to court to see who has the better lawyer!

The wheels of justice turn slowly, and it is very expensive to keep the machinery going. A judge decides the outcome, which is subject to appeal and additional investments of time, energy, and of course money. In the end there is a winner and a loser, or possibly two losers after all the bills have been paid.

In addition to the long time frame and high expense, litigation has other drawbacks. The outcome is uncertain and beyond the control of the parties — it is very risky. People in business like to reduce risk, not expose themselves to it. Litigation is a public process, and the decision is usually a matter of public record. Most people don't like airing their dirty laundry in public. The decision is handed down by a judge (or possibly a jury). While a judge may be an expert on the law, he may not be that knowledgeable about the substance of the dispute — there may be people who are more qualified to settle the matter. Finally, the confrontational nature of the legal process usually destroys whatever relationship the parties may have enjoyed.

For these reasons, there is a growing trend in many jurisdictions to require parties to first attempt to resolve their dispute by other means. When the parties arrive in court for their pre-trial hearing the judge will ask them if they have tried mediation. If they haven't, he will say "Go down the hall to room 2-C and spend an hour with the mediator." As the impact of the uncertainty of the outcome and exorbitant expense sinks in, the parties usually find they can agree to a settlement after all.

Of course, you don't have to wait for the judge to send you to mediation. You and your counterpart can agree to mediation or arbitration before either party decides to litigate. Going to court is a serious and expensive matter, with dire ramifications for your relationship. It should be used only as a last resort.

 Danger Zone

Litigants often choose a tough lawyer to make the other side pay. Unfortunately, highly confrontational lawyers are not always interested in resolving disputes amicably.

Mediation

Mediation is a less formal process than litigation. The rules of evidence and procedure are greatly relaxed, and lawyers are optional. It is quick and inexpensive. There is no judge or jury; rather, an impartial third party tries to facilitate an agreement between the disputing parties. The parties can choose to reach an agreement or not; no decision is imposed upon them. However, the mediator's skill in negotiation and dispute resolution, combined with her people skills, can often help the parties overcome their differences and reach an acceptable solution.

The beauty of mediation is its win-win philosophy. The parties are usually emotional and looking to beat their counterpart. (Remember, they may have been on their way to court a few minutes earlier.) Their attorneys are trained to be adversarial and are looking to justify their fees by giving their client a resounding victory, perhaps destroying their opponent in the process. However, the mediator is trained to look for win-win solutions that others may overlook. She is often able to help the parties reach a win-win agreement, or at least an acceptable compromise. The provisions of the agreement are confidential. The parties may well leave the room on good terms, with their relationship intact.

Arbitration

Like mediation, arbitration is a relatively quick, inexpensive, and informal alternative to litigation. However, there are a few important differences. The arbitrator, or the panel of arbitrators, is usually an expert in the field. For example, in a dispute between a general contractor and a subcontractor in a construction matter, the arbitrators may have experience in engineering, construction or project management. They are better able to understand the intricacies of the dispute and can render a more informed decision than a judge.

Unlike mediation, the arbitrator's decision is usually binding. The parties agree to submit their case to an expert and abide by his decision, rather than take their chances with a judge. In fact, many contracts provide that disputes will be submitted for arbitration rather than litigation. There is usually no appeal from an arbitrator's award. As with mediation, the decision is private and the parties' relationship may well survive the proceedings.

Fast Fact

The overwhelming majority of lawsuits are settled out of court.

Of the three methods of dispute resolution, mediation is most useful in keeping with the spirit of a win-win negotiation. In fact, mediation is a form of negotiation, with the guidance of an expert. Avoid litigation and the spectre of a lose-lose result if at all possible.

Star Tips for wrapping up negotiations

1. Do not simply put the agreement out of your mind after the concluding handshake.

2. Take detailed notes throughout the negotiation to guard against memory differences or misunderstandings.

3. Use your notes to draft memoranda at key points during a lengthy negotiation.

4. Prepare a draft of the final agreement you hope to negotiate before you even begin negotiating. This helps you remain focused on your interests and allows you to evaluate the final result.

5. Maintain control over the final agreement by offering to draft it yourself.

6. Read every draft of the agreement carefully.

7. Follow up to make sure the agreement is implemented as planned.

8. Beware of nibbles — last-minute attempts to extract additional concessions.

9. Consider a post-settlement settlement to make a good agreement even better.

10. Bring in a mediator to resolve disputes quickly and cheaply. Go to court only as a last resort.

MORE WIN-WIN
NEGOTIATING WISDOM

*"When the only tool you have is a hammer,
every problem begins to resemble a nail."*
Abraham Maslow

We have looked at the mindset and behaviours of win-win negotiators. We have seen how they prepare and gather information, how they set the stage for negotiation, how they use tactics and counter-tactics. In this final chapter, I have a few more important lessons to share with you, and a few warnings that you need to be aware of. Let's look at several important pieces of win-win negotiating wisdom.

Framing issues

Two people can look at the same situation and interpret it differently. One sees the glass as half empty, the other as half full. One sees a number as six, the other as nine. One sees a risk, the other an opportunity to gain. How you see it depends on the lens through which you view the world, or your frame.

A frame is an arbitrary reference point that influences the way a person views a situation. While people will usually adopt a frame without giving it much thought, they can be swayed to adopt another frame. This ability to shape another's perceptions is too powerful to ignore. Consequently, a win-win negotiator thinks about how issues are framed.

Aha! Moment

By framing an issue or wording a proposal a certain way, I can influence the way my counterpart responds.

For example, most people tend to feel more strongly about avoiding a loss than working for a gain. People in a loss-minimising frame of mind will try harder and risk more to avoid the loss. You can exploit this mindset by playing to their fears, by saying, "It would be a shame to miss out on this deal after all we've put into it."

People in a gain-maximising frame, on the other hand, are more conservative and more likely to accept a moderate gain than to fight hard for a more advantageous settlement. They are easier to negotiate with. The upshot of all this is that you should encourage your counterpart to adopt a gain-maximising frame. You can influence her by emphasising what she stands to gain if you are able to reach an agreement, rather than what she may lose if you don't.

You can frame issues in other ways, such as fair/unfair, big/small, traditional/cutting edge, and so on. Just remember that the frame needs to be believable, so being able to justify it will help you.

You may be familiar with the story of Tom Sawyer whitewashing his Aunt Polly's fence. One fine sunny morning Aunt Polly assigned Tom this unpleasant chore. As Tom toiled away, other kids interrupted their play to tease him. Tom pretended not to be bothered, and told the others it wasn't *work*, it was *fun*. After all, it's not every day you get the chance to whitewash a fence.

It wasn't long before the other boys were begging for a turn with the brush. Tom expressed doubt as to whether to let others share in his fun, which made them even more eager to do it. Soon, all the boys in the neighbourhood were lining up for a turn, and trading their prized possessions for the privilege! Tom relaxed in the shade enjoying his windfall while the others completed his chore.

Tom Sawyer was able to persuade others to do an unpleasant task by framing it in a positive way. The other boys adopted his frame and agreed to his proposal.

Make it easy for them to say "yes"

When my daughter was a toddler she would follow me into the storeroom and pick up tools, light bulbs and other items I didn't want her to play with. Asking her to leave the things alone didn't work; she didn't see any advantage in agreeing to my proposal. So I then asked her to close the door for me. For a one-year-old, closing the door sounded like more fun than holding a hammer. It took some mental effort, but I had thought of a way to make it easy for her to say "yes".

I like to think I am more powerful than my daughter and can demand her compliance. By traditional measures of power such as size and strength, I am more powerful than she is. A lot of negotiators like to think this way. However, it is counterproductive. It causes resentment and harms the relationship. Wouldn't it be better to gain someone's willing and enthusiastic co-operation rather than her grudging compliance?

Put yourself in the other party's shoes. She won't do anything simply because you want her to. She will only do things because she wants to. Try to understand what she wants, bearing in mind that she may not want the same things you want.

 Aha! Moment

I can craft my proposal so my counterpart will want to say "yes".

You're not just negotiating with him

Most negotiators focus on the person sitting across the table from them. They may even tailor their words and approach to this person's personality, negotiating style, and other individual characteristics. This sounds good, but it isn't enough. The person you're looking at is often just the tip of the iceberg.

There's more to consider than just the person sitting at the table with you. Your counterpart has other constituents to answer to. He will need to gain their buy-in. For example, his boss will be interested in the outcome, and he will be concerned about what his boss will think. You will have to justify your proposals to your counterpart, and help him justify his actions to his stakeholders. Try to identify who these stakeholders are, what their interests are, and how you can win their support.

Consider your counterpart negotiating a purchase from you. His boss is concerned about the price. Your counterpart is concerned about his boss. If you want him to agree to a higher price, help him justify to himself and his boss why your product is worth more. Help make him a hero in his boss's eyes.

Negotiating by telephone or e-mail

Many people ask me if they should negotiate face-to-face, by telephone, or through e-mail. In many instances the answer will be dictated by considerations of cost, location, timing and convenience. In other instances, you will have a choice.

Negotiating face-to-face is more formal, but fosters better communication and understanding. After all, you have the benefit of observing facial expression, body language, and other non-verbal cues. As a result, face-to-face negotiation is more likely to result in a win-win outcome. This makes it suitable for negotiating more substantial matters.

Many negotiations are now conducted by e-mail. E-mail communication is more likely to be misinterpreted than face-to-face or telephone communication, but it might be the best choice for small matters, or where there are time, travel or cost constraints. However, negotiating by e-mail is least likely to result in a win-win outcome.

Negotiating by telephone is a quick, low cost option. This channel ranks in between face-to-face meetings and e-mail exchanges in terms of clarity of communication. It is good for routine matters, or those not weighty enough to justify face-to-face contact.

There are a few other advantages to telephone negotiations:

• They take less time than face-to-face meetings. Sometimes a simple face-to-face negotiation is drawn out simply to justify the time and effort required to travel to your counterpart's office.

• It is easier to say "no" over the phone. The telephone provides a buffer and eliminates the need to look into the eyes of the disappointed party.

• The telephone is less intimidating than face-to-face meetings for less assertive negotiators, so this helps the less powerful party. Disappointed eyes are bad enough, but an intimidating face is even harder to handle!

• It gives substance and logic more weight relative to style and form. There may be some pomp and circumstance in a face-to-face meeting, whereas a telephone negotiation allows you to cut to the chase.

Fast Fact

The more important the negotiation, the more desirable it becomes to negotiate face-to-face.

Concessions

Almost every negotiation requires concessions before you can reach an agreement. A concession is when you moderate your position to move closer to your counterpart. For example, raising the amount of your offer, lowering your asking price, or offering other value to your counterpart are all forms of concession. It is important that you make concessions the right way.

Suppose you are a buyer negotiating to purchase an item. You are prepared to pay up to $1,000 more than your initial offer. How should you pattern your concessions?

First of all, don't offer a concession right away. If you appear too willing to give concessions, your negotiating partner will assume you will give more as the negotiation progresses. Make your partner work for it. The harder he works, the more he values the result.

Secondly, do not offer a large portion of your $1,000 at once. This also signals that more concessions are on the way. Start with a modest concession, with later concessions of diminishing size. As your concessions get smaller, you signal that you are approaching your bottom line.

Thirdly, avoid giving a concession without getting one in return. If you are asked for a concession, ask for something in exchange. For example, you could say "I could do X for you if you will do Y for me." If you do find yourself making a unilateral concession to get a stalled negotiation moving again, make sure you don't give another one until your counterpart concedes something to you. If you give two concessions in a row, your counterpart will ask for a third, and a fourth and a fifth.

Aha! Moment

The way I pattern my concessions will send important signals to my counterpart and influence his responses.

Fast Fact

Make your concessions sparingly, taper them as the negotiation progresses, and always ask for something in return for every concession you give.

Ultimatums

An ultimatum is a demand that something be done by a certain deadline, with a punishment for non-compliance. It is a threat that may or may not be believed by the recipient, and may or may not be carried out by the issuer. There are four ways in which an ultimatum can play out:

- **Successful bluff.** The issuer doesn't mean it, but the recipient believes it. The issuer got lucky.

- **Failed bluff.** The issuer doesn't mean it, and the recipient doesn't believe it. The issuer loses credibility.

- **Successful ultimatum.** The issuer means it, and the recipient believes it. The issuer gets his way.

- **Failed ultimatum.** The issuer means it, but the recipient doesn't believe it. The issuer must follow through with the threat or risk losing credibility.

Issuing an ultimatum is a risky gambit. The result will depend in part on the resolve of the issuer and in part on whether the recipient believes it. The issuer may be more or less convincing, but he cannot be sure how the recipient will respond.

When you say, "That's my final offer" or "Take it or leave it," you put yourself into a corner. If you follow through with your ultimatum, you may lose a deal you wanted. If you don't follow through, you lose credibility. Either way, you offend the other party.

 Danger Zone

> Do not give an ultimatum unless you are sure of yourself and really mean it. Explain why you are forced to insist on it — people like to hear a reason. Make it believable.

If you must issue an ultimatum, give a gentle one rather than a harsh one. "Take it or leave it" is abrupt and insensitive to the other party. He will be offended. You can convey the same either/or message in a much nicer way. For example: "It's the best I can do; work with me." This does not sound like an ultimatum; it sounds like a plea for help. The recipient will not be offended, and may even be sympathetic.

Give your ultimatum with a less desirable alternative so your counterpart can choose. For example, "I know you could probably get your asking price eventually, but this is all we have in our budget." The recipient might not like the prospect of waiting for a better offer, so your gentle ultimatum sounds appealing.

What should you do if your counterpart issues you an ultimatum? You have a few options:

- Offer a partial agreement and try to negotiate further.

- Make a counter offer. It is rarely either A or B. Offer them C — they might accept.

- Ignore it and continue talking. Suggest they think about it and get back to you later. This reduces the pressure to follow through on their threat to maintain credibility, and allows them a face-saving way to back down. The more time that passes, the less likely they will follow through with their threat.

- Walk away, but be civil. Circumstances change, and you may find yourself back at the negotiating table with them later. Or you may exercise your Plan B.

Dealing with an impasse

You will frequently reach a point in a negotiation where you get stuck. Neither side wants to budge, progress is halted, and frustration mounts. You may wonder whether you will ever reach agreement. What can you do when you reach an impasse? Here are some suggestions:

1. Most progress in a negotiation usually occurs in the final stages. Recognise that an impasse is common and does not signal failure. Accept it as a hurdle that can and will be overcome.

2. Focus on your interests, and help your counterpart focus on his. It is natural to get distracted by minor issues in the heat of bargaining. Refocusing on interests and priorities can get the negotiation back on track.

3. Look for creative ways to add value. Explore options that have been overlooked. As a negotiation proceeds you learn new information, which that can lead you to other possible solutions.

4. Offer to grant a small concession, but demand one in return. A small movement can get things rolling again.

5. Focus the negotiation on smaller or easier items. As you reach agreement on some minor points, you build momentum that can carry you forward.

6. Change the dynamics of the negotiation. A change in players and personalities can jumpstart a stalled negotiation.

7. You might also change the environment. Different surroundings can change the atmosphere and put you back on track.

8. Take a time out. Review your strategy and allow emotions to cool down. Sometimes taking a break to relax and clear your head can work wonders.

9. Agree to impose a period of silence. This is not the same as taking a break. Everyone stays in the room, they just don't say a word for five or ten minutes. During this time all kinds of thoughts creep into our minds, causing both sides to moderate their expectations.

10. You could also impose a deadline. In many negotiations most of the progress is made in the final stages, as the deadline approaches. Sometimes, time pressure is just the kick in the pants the parties need to get things moving again.

11. Ask your counterpart for his agreement. Sometimes it is just as simple as asking. If he says "yes," great! If he says "no," ask "why not?" Listen carefully to his answer, address his concerns, and set forth the remaining steps needed to conclude an agreement.

12. If things seem hopeless, consider bringing in an impartial third party. More often than not, a good mediator can help the parties reach an agreement.

13. Finally, be prepared to walk away if necessary. Just be sure you are not bluffing, and that you have somewhere to walk away to. This takes guts, but it may apply pressure on the other side to be more flexible.

 Aha! Moment

There are many things I can do to get a stalled negotiation moving again.

Fast Fact

An impasse need not be the end of the line. Be persistent and you can put the negotiation back on track.

Five negative negotiating behaviours

In Chapter 2 we saw that win-win negotiators engage in certain behaviours that help bring about win-win solutions: they ask questions, listen, empathise, consider and explain, and think creatively. They also avoid these five behaviours that negatively affect negotiations.

Personal attacks

Negotiations can get intense. Long hours, incompatible demands, unmet expectations, personality and cultural clashes, and lack of progress can frustrate the participants. Tempers rise. Harsh words are exchanged. Things can get personal.

The average negotiator, when attacked, is likely to defend himself and then launch a counterattack against the other side. These attacks and counterattacks can spiral out of control and cause emotions to flare and egos to bruise. They make any agreement, let alone a win-win, less likely.

A win-win negotiator will not launch a personal attack, nor will he respond to such an attack in kind. However, everyone makes mistakes. We also experience misunderstandings, use language that may be interpreted in ways we didn't intend, and inadvertently cause offence.

A win-win negotiator will defuse an emotionally charged situation and stop it from escalating. The simple act of apologising can do wonders. An apology followed by a question shows concern for the other party and allows him the opportunity to be heard. For example:

> *"I'm sorry, I didn't mean to seem unreasonable. Is there anything else you would like to add?"*

Too many arguments

Most negotiators offer as many arguments as they can think of to support their position. They think that the more arguments they have, the stronger their cause. It's as if each argument they advance has a certain amount of weight, and they try to outweigh their counterpart!

In fact, advancing too many arguments dilutes the strength of your main point. People can only remember a few points, and anything more is wasted. Worse, they will focus their attention on the weakest link and use it to dismiss your entire proposal.

Win-win negotiators advance one or two strong arguments in support of their proposal, rather than a multitude of weaker arguments. Don't give your counterpart anything weak to seize upon. Quality of argument prevails over quantity.

 Fast Fact

One solid argument is more effective than numerous weaker ones.

Abrasive comments

Win-win negotiators do not make patronising, value-laden comments about how fair they are being to their counterpart. Such comments suggest the offeree would be unreasonable not to agree, and can escalate into a vicious cycle of attacks and counterattacks. For example:

"I believe you will find our offer to be most generous" sounds like a perfectly reasonable way to encourage the other party to accept your offer. However, the other party is likely to interpret it as: *"I'm doing you a huge favour and you'd be a fool to reject it!"*

Think about the ways in which your counterpart can take your comments. Do not use language that may be insulting, such as:

"That's ridiculous!"

"Are you out of your mind?"

"Don't be such a cheapskate."

Needless to say, you must avoid obscenity, ethnic slurs, and other offensive language.

Overconfidence

Confidence born of solid preparation is a good thing. Overconfidence is not. Overestimating the strength of your position can close your mind to new information and other options. Make a realistic assessment of the situation and watch for new information that may have a bearing on the outcome. Overconfidence can blind you to new information as well as dangers.

Overconfidence can also make you too rigid. Be prepared to change your assumptions, strategy, and even your expectations in light of new developments. Win-win negotiators are confident, but not *too* confident. They are also flexible.

Losing focus

Having invested time, money, effort and ego into a negotiation, you may feel pressure to reach an agreement, even if it is not to your advantage. Focus on your objective, not on what you have already lost. Win-win negotiators understand that whatever has been invested is gone, and no deal is still better than a bad deal.

It is never too late to walk away. Focus on your interests, remember your Plan B, and remain cordial — you may be able to resume negotiations later.

 Try This

Write down your bottom line as determined when you were preparing to negotiate. Refer to it when you feel pressure. Also refer to your Plan B and refocus on your objective.

There is much more to learn about becoming a win-win negotiator. No doubt you will learn some lessons from mistakes you will make. Remember that doing so is infinitely better than *not* learning from your mistakes. Take heart in the knowledge that even world-class negotiators make mistakes. Becoming a win-win negotiator is a life-long journey, but it is a rewarding one.

Fast Fact

Negotiation is a game. Preparation allows both you and your counterpart to win. As you learn to play the game better, you will find that your skill has a greater impact on your results, and chance plays a smaller role. These skills will serve you well throughout your life.

Star Tips for further developing your win-win negotiating skills and mindset

1. Frame issues thoughtfully. This will influence the way others interpret and respond to situations.

2. Make it easy for your counterpart to say "yes".

3. Consider your counterpart's constituents and help him win their buy-in.

4. Weigh the pros and cons of conducting a given negotiation face-to-face, by telephone, or through e-mail.

5. Make concessions sparingly, taper them as the negotiation progresses, and demand something in return for every concession you make.

6. Give an ultimatum only if you are certain, and do it gently.

7. Redouble your efforts in the face of an impasse. It is not unusual for a negotiation to get bogged down, and most progress occurs towards the end.

8. Avoid personal attacks, abrasive language, and other negative behaviours.

9. Advance one or two strong arguments for your proposal rather than a multitude of weaker ones.

10. Accept that you will make mistakes just as world-class negotiators do, and continue honing your win-win negotiating skills throughout your lifetime.

INDEX

ABOUT THE AUTHOR

David Goldwich is a professional speaker and trainer specialising in the area of persuasive communication, including negotiation, influence and persuasion, assertiveness, conflict management, and storytelling in business.

David has MBA and JD degrees and practised law in the United States for over a decade, arguing before judges and advocating before government and community bodies. David is trained as a mediator and has experience managing a small business.

Recognising that lawyers perpetuate rather than solve problems, David began training to help people perform better, both on the job and off. David's use of stories, his sense of humour, wealth of experience, and his passion, enable him to deliver breakthrough changes at all levels of the organisation.

David is author of the book *Why Did the Chicken Cross the Road?: Lessons in Effective Communication*. He has also published a collection of humourous essays entitled *Getting Into Singapore: A Guide for Expats and Kaypoh Singaporeans*. He has written numerous articles on business and communication issues, and is a frequent guest on radio shows.

Born and raised in Miami, Florida, USA, David has been living in Singapore and working throughout Asia since 1999.

 **ST Training Solutions**

Success Skills Series

ST Training Solutions, based in Singapore, offers a wide range of popular, practical training programmes conducted by experienced, professional trainers. As CEO, Shirley Taylor takes a personal interest in working closely with trainers to ensure that each workshop is full of valuable tools, helpful guidelines and powerful action steps that will ensure a true learning experience for all participants. Some of the workshops offered are:

Powerful Business Writing Skills
Energise your E-mail Writing Skills
Success Skills for Secretaries and Support Staff
Successful Business Communication Skills
Making Great Connections
Creativity at Work
Speaking without Fear
Professional People Skills
Activate your Listening Skills
Win-Win Negotiation Skills
Emotional Intelligence at Work
Business Etiquette and Professional Protocol
Dealing with Difficult People and Situations
Achieving Peak Performance by Improving your Memory
Projecting a Professional Image
Writing in Response to Complaints
Writing Effective Minutes

Shirley Taylor is also host of a very popular annual conference called ASSAP — the Asian Summit for Secretaries and Admin Professionals — organised in April each year by ST Training Solutions.

Find out more about ST Training Solutions at www.shirleytaylortraining.com. Visit www.STSuccessSkills.com for additional resources.